Finding Blessings in a Cursed Life:

Mance Cuplov

Written by Lenny Giardino

Edited by Amy Kulow-Taylor

Decency Publishing

Author's Foreword

What is Trauma?

My name is Lenny Giardino. I am currently the Superintendent of Schools for a large non-profit in Upstate New York that serves students with moderate to complex disabilities from New York City to Buffalo. For the past 30 years, I have worked in the Human Service and Education fields. I have worked in both large cities and small communities across the United States.

My career has been diverse, working with many people across the spectrum of humanity itself. As part of that diversity, I learned that we as a nation have a vast amount of wants and needs that is guided by our personal experiences. From this, I have also learned the role that trauma plays in shaping the lives of many individuals.

Early trauma in a person's life combined with a high frequency of traumatic events can be devastating for many individuals, sometimes without them understanding the impact. Some people may only have a few traumatic events in their lives, spread out across time, allowing them the chance to properly process and heal in between. Others have a pattern of successive traumas that start in early childhood and continue for many years, draining their wellbeing, causing a lifetime of pain and suffering.

Some may have a limited view of trauma, thinking it solely consists of acts such as gun violence, domestic disputes, and bullying. While these are indeed traumatic events, most people I have worked with are impacted by systemic trauma, in that they are a part of a system that fails to provide a safe environment.

One example of systemic trauma is poverty. Poorer communities lack access to safe and reliable housing, as well as fresh and healthy food choice. There is extreme violence in their neighborhoods. Schools provide substandard educational opportunities. People in these situations are experiencing more than isolated traumatic events—trauma is a part of their daily life.

As part of this daily trauma, people may self-medicate to cope with their trauma, which can then lead to physical and verbal aggression. Long-term exposure to aggression can lead to dysfunction and mental health issues, causing the cycle of trauma to continue.

I have served people that suffer from mental illness in many different capacities. There is no doubt in my mind that mental illness is impacted by trauma. There was a time during the winter that I gave out blankets to people that were living under bridges in Upstate New York. Some of my colleagues that helped that day asked, "Why can't they go to the shelters where it is warm?" If you have extreme trauma, the bridge feels safer than the shelter. For them, they are paralyzed by the pain of traumatic life experiences.

Overcoming Trauma

What inspires me to write books like this one is seeing people overcoming trauma and moving past the paralysis it can cause. When they acknowledge their trauma and learn from it, they find a path to healing. Some may connect to that path of healing by finding inspiration in others that experienced similar trauma.

For people recovering from a lifetime of trauma, it can be very difficult for them to talk about it, but others can find inspiration from their stories of resilience. When a person shares their story about trauma, it both helps them to process their trauma while also helping others to cope and regain hope in their lives.

Reading this book may be difficult for some people. Some people prefer live in the shadows and not acknowledge the truth of trauma. Yet, we need to be honest about the world we live in and honest about ourselves. There is no shame or embarrassment in talking about our own trauma, nor should there be. Shying away from the truth only leads to misconceptions, and misconceptions can lead to more harm.

A few years ago, I wrote my first book on the topic, titled *Finding Blessings in Cursed Life*, a story of early childhood trauma and domestic abuse. At the book signings, there were people who waited to talk to us after everyone left, and they told us their own stories. Once someone feels comfortable talking about their past, at that very moment, real change can happen.

For this reason, I decide to write another *Finding Blessings in a Cursed Life* book based on a very special person who has a unique story to be told. I truly believe after reading about Mance Cuplov, you will find overcoming trauma is something we can do once we find the inspiration to bring about change in our lives. Mance and I both hope her story brings hope and resilience into your life.

Meeting Mance Cuplov

My first meeting of Mance Cuplov was in Chadwicks, New York, where Mance works as a Teacher Assistant in a program I oversee. One day when we were talking, she started to tell me her experiences growing up in communist Bosnia, which I found fascinating. It was the beginning of a wonderful friendship. Together, we decided to write a book about her life experiences.

Having lived in a communist nation is an interesting aspect of Mance's life. Communist nations are built on laws and rituals that are almost religious in nature, but one where the religion is focused on living gods versus mystical figures. From a communist leader like Josef Tito to the classroom teacher, children were taught reverence very early in their life.

Mance described how her school groomed students to be communist and indoctrinated with the party's beliefs. They were given red membership books. There were ceremonies where people were given a red carnation as they became a member of the communist party. While religion was mostly non-existent in Yugoslavia, there were mosques and churches. Children from religious families would typically declare "no" when asked if they wanted to join the communist party, and some families were shunned if they chose not to be communists.

When the Berlin Wall fell and communism collapsed in the Eastern Bloc, former province of Yugoslavia fell apart. Hidden in the shadows of communism were conflicting ethnic and religious differences that would worsen when communism was gone. In an effort to gain control of Bosnia, Serbs rounded up Bosnian Muslims, executing them in mass numbers. When you learn about all that Mance has experienced, it is difficult to fathom how she survived so many years of abuse, neglect, and suffering.

It was hard for Mance to start discussing her feelings and emotions in a constructive manner. We had to work on building trust first before we could talk about her life. This meant giving Mance full reign over our visits when we started to work on this book. A pattern emerged where she would go to a dark place, but then would suddenly recover from it with food and storytelling. We spent well over two years unravelling her experiences.

The first time I went to visit Mance at her home in Utica, NY, I was welcomed in and given a tour. She lives in a grand old home in the inner city. The house is meticulously decorated with artwork and influenced by history. I sensed there was a story behind much of the home's décor as the artwork seemed to tell a story about Mance's life.

In Mance's world, food is both love and part of the story. She served me a home-cooked Bosnian meal consisting of meat pie and a smoked Bosnian meat platter. I sensed that there were many parts to Mance that I would learn on the journey to writing the book together, and that we were only just beginning.

For our second visit, Mance served me another amazing meal, despite struggling with her personal health and wearing a brace for a back injury. She shared with me the pain she felt that day. For Mance, pain reminds her of every punch, every pain, and every loss that she experienced in life. Many of these pains were experienced in a concentration camp, and then as a refugee. At one point during our second visit, she discussed her hunger pangs while being pregnant in her homeland—pangs of pain that never left her.

During this visit with Mance, I learned she was an old soul, and much wiser than one would conclude from her vibrant personality. At times, she behaves like an 18-year-old. She is full of life and brings a smile to anyone that gets to know her.

On our third visit, Mance was struggling with finding out that her one-year-old grandchild in Sarajevo had a serious bacterial infection. Later, she would discover his illness was related to the COVID-19 outbreak. At the time, cases had not yet become prevalent in the United States.

In addition to worrying about her grandson, Mance was worried about her daughter-in-law, the mother of her grandson. Her daughter-in-law's boss was not a nice man, and in Eastern Europe, you cannot do much about a rotten boss. He had very little compassion for Mance's daughter-in-law tending to her sick son. When Mance's daughter-in-law attempted to call in to work, she was told, "You need to get to work. What am I going to do with you at home? I need an employee, not you." Months later, we learned that she was fired from her job due to similar absences.

I offered to cancel our meeting, but Mance still wanted me to come over, demonstrating the resiliency she developed through her trauma. Her resiliency is a reoccurring theme throughout our time together, and it is important for people reading this book to recognize resiliency in the face of true trauma. Drama and trauma are often conflated in our country. People sometimes perceive drama as being traumatic, but these events pale in comparison to true extreme traumatic experiences. It is our hope that reading about Mance's life will help people understand the difference between the two.

For my fourth visit, I was greeted with some amazing lamb chops. As Mance had not been feeling well, we had cancelled several prior meetings. She also continued to worry about her grandchild, as well as her son, who struggles with substance abuse. This visit was the first time she would talk about her fears over her son's safety, but I would soon learn more.

During my fifth visit, Mance was upset with her son. He was not supporting her daughter in-law with their child's fight to survive in the hospital. Mance was secretly providing for his family as he cannot. As long as he struggles with substance abuse, he cannot love nor care for himself, much less care for others.

For Mance, the pain of Bosnia never goes away. Even though she is thousands of miles away, the pain is just as real as if she was still there. Pain, guilt, and suffering are a part of trauma, and are obstacles for living a blessed life. However, they are only that—obstacles. And obstacles can be overcome.

The following weeks had ebbs and flows. People who are recovering from severe trauma have days when they need to provide themselves respite. This is the case for Mance, and sometimes myself as well.

The Impact of COVID-19

Life provides us reminders of our past. During the writing and interview process, COVID-19 hit New York State. Our state was an epicenter for the virus. For most of us, we experienced a world shutdown for the first time. For Mance, it was a dark reminder of her experiences during the war in Yugoslavia— loved ones disappearing, confinement inside, and the lack of freedom to live life as we once did without fear.

The emptiness of our area during the pandemic provided Mance a reminder of how life can change at a moment's notice. The best and worst of people would appear as a reaction to the trauma of being quarantined. During any crisis, there is a shortsightedness to people that resembles the culture of communism. Power structures fear losing control over their subordinates. The loss of control scares people, and they cannot adjust to a new normal.

But Mance was never afraid of the pandemic. Her reaction was to go back to work. When she saw people panic, she wanted to help. She could give people perspective, as she had been through much worse. It is better to exercise control over what we can versus succumbing to fear of the things we cannot. For Mance, what she could control was volunteering to help others during this process.

Life experiences provide memories that our brain can draw upon and use to create pathways forward when we need it. In the case of the pandemic, pathways to acceptance opened up for those that had already experienced trauma versus pathways closing for those who had not. Mance is a living example of this cognitive learning theory.

A year later, I revisited this passage. The crisis has changed, and now we struggle with two political factions—the vaccinated and the unvaccinated. Each believe their rights are being infringed upon by the other. Emotions are running high. It is our hope that Mance's story helps to remind our readers that divided we fall, united we shall succeed.

Mance's Story

My Parents

The story of my parents is one that does not have a happy ending. My relationship with my parents was a relationship that was abusive, both verbally and physically. This is not to say that I do not love my parents. I love them dearly.

My mother was born in central Bosnia in the little town of Fojncia. She was the fifth of seven children—six girls and one boy. My mother was beautiful. She was 15 years old when she married my father.

Growing up, she had a very difficult childhood. My grandfather was a farmer who owned lots of land. Back then, everything was done by hand. Hard labor from every daughter helped provide for them on the farm. They had their own house thanks to the labors of the family unit.

My mother was in charge of the barn and cows, which meant she was in charge of making all the milk products. My mother claimed she kept it so clean in her barn, you could sit under the cow and not get dirty.

My father came from Rogatica. He came from a smaller family which consisted of one sister and his mother. He never knew his father. His father left the family, which may have played a role in how my father behaved.

As a child, he became familiar with German soldiers during World War II. When they came through, they would stop and talk to the villagers. He remembers the German soldiers as being very nice to the kids in the village.

My father was a mechanic. He was also a wild man. Prior to meeting my mother, my father had a motorcycle accident and broke his back. Shortly before his accident, he had witnessed a friend in a horrible accident that eventually led to his friend's demise. At the time, he told his sister, "Oh my God, if I ever had that kind of accident, I would kill myself." Seven days later, he crippled himself in a similar serious accident. Irony was very much a part of my father's life.

After the accident, he was put in a bathtub in a full body cast to heal his back. My father fought his way back to good health, and he was able to walk many years later with a cane. He was a fighter.

He spent many years in the hospital in Sarajevo. They then transferred him to the Muscular Dystrophy Center for Rehabilitation in Fojnica, where he ended up meeting my mother. My mom was bringing bottles of milk to the hospital as part of her responsibilities on the farm. One day, while my dad was in rehabilitation and my mother was bringing milk to the hospital kitchen, she saw my father sitting on a bench.

Over time, as my father started to gain back some mobility from the accident, he would go to sit in the park and talk to my mother. My mother fell in love with my father—or maybe she felt sorry for him being disabled. Sometimes, love and sadness get mixed up. My father and mother dated for a short time, and then they married.

My dad was 18 years older than my mom. When they met, she was dating another man her age. After meeting my father, she rejected the man she was dating, and he was heartbroken. When he learned that she agreed to marry my father, he said to her, "Please don't. Please marry me." But she turned down his proposal.

My mom went to the farm to tell her father that she was going to marry my father. But she couldn't find my grandfather as he was out working the land. Meanwhile, my father had come to the farm by bus to pick up my mother.

My grandmother and aunt tried to stop my mother from getting married. They searched the fields for my grandfather, knowing how he would feel about the marriage. When they found him and told him, my grandfather was so angry, he left everything in the field, including the horses. He ran back to the house to stop my mom from getting married—he did not want her to marry a disabled man at such a young age

My mother was told how upset my grandfather was, and that she had better run away because my grandfather was ready to kill somebody. She hid from my grandfather and snuck on the bus. This decision shaped my mother's life permanently, leading to her eventual death.

It was the bus ride to hell. The ride took five hours, so she sang to pass the time, but the other riders were so serious. She did not realize at the time, but that ride would the last time she felt truly happy.

My mom arrived with my father in the city of Rogatica. They moved into a tiny house next to my father's sister. My mother was welcomed into my father's family, although everyone acknowledged she was too young to be married. In their eyes, my mother needed to grow up more before she could be a wife.

My father had a temper, which my mother had to deal with alone, being isolated from her family. She was such a beautiful lady, which caused extreme jealousy in my father. I remember that my father would become jealous over simple things. Our neighbor could walk by and say hello, and my father would beat my mother over it.

My father eventually sold the tiny home to his sister. Our family moved into an apartment that was owned by a man that owned a bakery. My dad also bought some land and started to build a house. In 1962, I was born in the bakery apartment. After my birth, we moved into the new house.

My father started to understand that his health was getting worse, while my mother was becoming even more beautiful. He was frugal to begin with, but then he starting to save money for himself, and only himself. My mom had to resort to hiding things so that she could have her own money as well.

One of the ways that my mother made money was by singing. My mother was an excellent singer. Her voice was so moving, sometimes, people would cry after hearing her. She was good enough to perform professionally, and so she would go to singing engagements that my father arranged for her. The only problem was, as singers often do, she would get compliments after her singing engagements, and this would lead to beatings when she went home. Eventually, my mother became tired of these beatings, and she stopped singing.

But despite no longer singing, the abuse continued. Over time, my father became more and more agitated, beating her for the slightest thing, like a neighbor walking by. One winter when my mother was 17, my father saw that some apples had spoiled, and he kicked her out of the house with my brother, who was a baby. It was a cold winter's night, and nobody would help her. There was no one in Rogatica she could turn to for help.

Separation and Abandonment

My mother started working in a factory that made children's clothing, which was a major issue for my father. He would spy on her at the factory, and then beat her when she got home. Again, she quit to try to appease my father. She had a knitting machine to make sweaters, so she then bought a sewing machine from a salesman to also make dresses, allowing her to work from home. Working from home meant fewer interactions with other people, which meant fewer beatings.

Ironically, though, working from home was what made my father's jealous fears come true. The salesman who sold her the sewing machine would spend time with her, teaching her how to use the machine. He was kind, and she fell in love with him.

When I was around 10 years old, my mom and dad decided to live apart in the same house. My mother could not get a divorce in a communist country since my father did not want a divorce. Separation was not an option either. My father was so angry at my mom, his hatred created a living hell for all of us.

One day, she met a man that drove by our house in an Audi. My mom was enamored by him. She would sit on the sofa and wait for him to drive by. When she would see him, she would meet him in the car and drive off. I don't know where they went— only that she met him in hiding, and sometimes she would come home bruised.

Even while separated and seeing the man with the Audi, my mom would have to ask my father's permission to buy shoes or clothes. It was upsetting to me that she was living like this. Walking between these two worlds with my father and my mother's boyfriend would impact both me and my mother. We answered to two men that wanted control over our lives.

Whenever the man with the Audi came by (and it was always random when he would come), my mother would drop everything and leave with him. She would run off at times when people were visiting, leaving me in charge to entertain her friends. I didn't know how to explain her random absences. Little did I know the entire neighborhood already knew what was going on and where my mom was going. It was so unpredictable and unsettling for me. I would feel angry over her abandoning me and my brother, but I was not allowed to express my feelings. I still feel resentful when I think about it.

I also resented my mother's lack of love and support. One time, a neighbor accused me of stealing fruit. I did not do it, but my mother did not defend me against the neighbor. Instead, my mother gave me a beating with a stick.

Another time, my neighbor's grapes became damaged. She told my mom that it was me and my friends who damaged her grapes. Again, I got in trouble and was beaten. The next day, that same neighbor came over to have coffee. My mom made me make the coffee for her and our neighbor.

The neighbor shared that she bought a pair of shoes that she had to hide from her husband, which she had left outside of our house. I wanted so badly to get even, so I spit in the coffee. Later, I peed in her new pair of shoes. At the time, I was feeling anger toward my neighbor for falsely accusing me of damaging her grapes. But deeper down, my real anger was toward my mother for not believing me, for beating me, and for abandoning me for the man in the Audi.

The Pains of Childhood

My parents were not tolerant of us when it came to our care. Being free from us and our complaints was their goal. There was an unwritten rule in our home that non-visible pains do not require a visit to the doctor. Instead, we would be given elixirs as an alternative to medical care.

My entire childhood consisted of extreme discomfort in my stomach. I would try to explain my pain to my parents, but they were so self-centered in their own misery, they ignored my pain, claiming it was in my head. My brother had similar pains in his back, and he received the same response from our parents.

One time, my brother was at our grandparents' house, and he became very ill. Our grandmother brought him to Sarajevo, where it was discovered that he had developed Hepatitis C. My brother had to stay in the hospital for the next three months. Even with the hospitalization, though, my father had no empathy for my brother's pain. Later in life, my father would not understand why we as his children did not trust him, and how that mistrust stemmed from not being cared for when we were young. As for my brother, he continued to have back pain throughout his life, which he would later discover were due to impacted kidney stones.

I would grow up knowing more about my parents than my parents would know about their own kids. I didn't understand then, but I have a better understanding now of my dad. His disability guided his anger. He was frustrated about his lot in life, and he took it out on others. His pain became our pain.

I also now understand my mother and why she couldn't fully care for us. The daily perils of abuse and neglect she experienced were the reasons for our neglect as children. She was unable to recognize how her pain affected all of us—she could only live through it. The fact that I could not help her and that her pain eventually led to her death is something I have to live with every day

Pticijak (Bird Hill)

There are some happy memories from my childhood. I lived near a forest, called Pticijak or Bird Hill, that had a cemetery dating back to the Turkish Empire. The old stones were accompanied by wild strawberries. It was an idyllic setting.

My mom and I would tan on the hill with her girlfriends and their kids. I would pick leaves from the trees that overlooked the city, bring them home, and press them (called herbarium or herbarij in my native country). I can still hear my mom yelling for me to come home while I was out on the hill.

I have some special memories of that hill. In Yugoslavia, May 1st is Labor Day. It was a communist tradition to celebrate on this day, and this continues today, even after the fall of Yugoslavia. People would gather and light fires. My mom and I would go to top of the hill, along with all my friends and family. The children would collect wood, and the neighbors would bring food.

My mom told me she wanted to be buried on Bird Hill. She picked a spot high on the hill. She wanted that spot because it looked over the city, and it is always sunny. I honored her wishes—Bird Hill is her final resting place.

Animal Refugees

Many times throughout my life, I have become involved in saving wildlife, both in Bosnia and in the United States. Rescuing animals is very important to me. I love my pets as much as I love my husband and my children!

When I was a little girl, I learned to love animals from my mother and father. One day, a German Shepherd came to the front of our house. He was wounded from being shot. My father took him in and named him Lassie, after the movie *Lassie's Coming Home.*

My parents earned the trust of the dog and trained him to protect the children. When they would leave, they would say, "Okay, Lassie, stay home and protect the kids," and the dog would go and sit in front of the door.

One day, a gentlemen walked by, and Lassie jumped over the fence and attacked the man. Lassie stopped, though, once my mom told him to stop. The gentlemen asked how Lassie ended up with us, and said he was Lassie's former owner. Then, the man admitted he was the one who had shot Lassie, and said, "I shot him once, and I am going to kill him!"

A few nights later, Lassie escaped his leash. He went to his former owner's home and got in a fight with the man's hunting dogs before coming back to our house. Lassie had remembered the hunting dogs were used to track him down when he was shot. The owner came back to our house with a gun and said, "Where is that dog?"

Lassie was very smart and knew how to outsmart the former owner. One day, Lassie was in a field and was shot at by the man. The man thought, once again, that Lassie was killed. In actuality, the dog was only playing dead. When it was safe, he came home.

My parents were so worried the former owner would try it again, they gave Lassie to a farmer who lived far away, so that Lassie would be safe. A week later, Lassie escaped from the farm and came to our house. The new owner, who was very nice, had to come get him. My mom felt like Lassie wanted our approval before he could leave with the new approval. Once I told him to his okay to go, Lassie went with his new owners.

From then on, I never stopped loving animals. A month before the holocaust started, I saved a cat that nobody wanted. It had many issues, including a broken jaw. One day, my father accidentally sat on the rescued cat. He said, "What the heck was that?" He was speechless when I explained about taking in the cat.

During the war, while in captivity, I asked the Chetnik soldiers if I could check on my father's house. When I approached the house, I saw the rescue cat. As I stared at the cat, extremists started killing people in front of their homes. A woman that was with me yelled, "Run!" Seeing the cat saved my life and was the reason why I escaped that day.

After the war, animals in the streets were rescued, and some lived with me in a home for refugees, which had a very special meaning for me. Sometimes, people without much trauma in their life fail to understand the importance of animals and what they can do for people with trauma. Veterans seek solace from horse therapy. Animals visit hospitals to give the infirmed hope because they provide much needed comfort that human beings cannot give. Animals can even restore the humanity that was once taken away by humans.

Kada

Growing up, we had a close family friend named Kada. Kada lived near our home, just down the street from us. She was born in our town and was a refugee from World War II. Kada lived in a small home built for refugees that survived the war.

Kada was born a boy named Avdo[1]. During the Bosnian war, Kada's mother hid her in a root cellar so that she would not have to go fight in the war. During the war, "Avdo" went missing. When the war was over, "Kada" magically appeared. There was story we were told that Avdo went under a rainbow and came out on the other side as Kada.

Kada would come over every night after sunset and stay until midnight, and my mother would feed her and help her however she could for 30 years, up until my mother's death. Kada was very important to my mother. In a sense, my mom adopted Kada as her own child, even though Kada an older woman—we knew Kada was older than my mom, but we never found out her actual age.

Kada caused tension between my mom and dad—my father was never happy that my mom was friends with Kada. He did not have much empathy for her circumstances. She came from a house without a bathroom, so she would smell like cat pee when she came over, which my father had a hard time ignoring. My mom would offer her a bath, but only if my father was not in the house.

We became comfortable leaving Kada alone in the house if we had things to do. Kada would also serve as my babysitter when

---

[1] Author's Notes—Kada was transgender. She would hide this from others, although people in the town had their suspicions. They would bully and mock Kada. This was very common in communist society.

my mother was absent. I could tell Kada my secrets, and she could tell me hers. Eventually, Kada trusted me enough to tell me her story, and about Avdo. She knew I would never betray her trust.

Kada became like a surrogate parent, especially with my mom going missing for increasingly longer periods of time. When I was upset with my mom, Kada would explain to me why my mom was behaving this way, and how it was rooted in fear. She helped me understand that my mother was a young woman who wanted to be loved by a man.

Kada and I would discuss my mother's estranged relationship with my dad, and my mom's boyfriend. Kada was honest with me about my mom's situation. My mother would tell Kada her worst experiences, and Kada would explain to me how this abuse impacted my mother. My mother was crucified by the people who lived in our community, and Kada understood the shame and embarrassment my mom felt during this time.

Kada also helped me understand that my father's anger came from being frustrated about his disability, which he could never admit. In Yugoslavia, men felt the pressure of being labeled as different by their peers. I could talk to Kada and trust her during this difficult time. She was my friend, psychiatrist, and confidant.[2]

---

[2] Authors Note—Part of living a cursed life and surviving the absence of a parent is to allow people into one's life to help with the healing process. While Mance knew as a fact that her mom loved her, Kada allowed her to process her feelings about the absence of her mother and would provide Mance with comfort. Lessons from Kada were a part of the learning process for Mance as a child.

Looking back, I understand why Kada could provide me comfort about my experiences. She understood what we were going through because of the verbal abuse she experienced due to her own struggles with identity, and the bullying that happens when people label you as different.

I learned the truth about Kada, and about Avdo, on the last day of her life. I wanted to visit Kada since she was ill. My mom told me that I should not make any faces when I saw Kada. I thought her comment was odd, but I went to see Kada anyway. I opened the door and saw Kada on her bed in a half-sitting position. As soon as Kada heard my voice, she tried to cover her head and face with a scarf. The scarf fell off, and instead of Kada in the bed, I saw an old man. She looked like the Wizard of Oz. Kada had a long white beard and hair to match. Because of her illness, she could not groom herself like she usually did, which allowed her natural beauty to show that day.

For me, Kada was like the Wizard of Oz every day. No matter what her lot was in life, she brought magic to everything she did. To me, she will always be Kada.

Kada was buried as she wished, as a woman. Her family honored her life. Today, her nieces and nephews are all well-educated doctors and professors. One is a famous professor in Sarajevo.

Kada's secret life was a lesson for me. We live in a cruel world. Gay, lesbian, and transgendered people often live in isolation because many humans lack empathy. I learned that truth via my own pain too. It is exposure to the human realities of isolation that help us understand the emptiness that fills people's soul.

Growing Up

As the years went on, I became angrier with my mother. In my mind, she should only be with one man. Why would she not forgive my father? I could not understand her unhappiness in her marriage nor that she was in love with another man. I was a part of the community that rejected my mother and was sympathetic only for my father. Even though my father was very abusive, I stood by him because I understood his hate came from my mother's inability to love him.

My mother and father only had the time to deal with their own misery, and so they struggled to care for us on an emotional level. For example, they never went to parent-teacher conferences at school. As I got older, I would tell the teacher that they were not going to come. There was a sense of shame that my parents would not go to school to meet with my teacher.

For me, becoming a teenager meant growing up quickly. I became a dancer, and being a dancer meant travel across Yugoslavia. But in order to dance, I would have to take care of my house chores first. My mom would make me clean the house and bake the bread. If my mom was not satisfied, I would not be allowed to go to dance training that day.

As part of my folklore dancing, I was asked to go to a competition in Libya to determine the best dance team, where we would dance in front of Moammar Khadafy. My father did not want to support me financially for the trip. When I asked my mom for help, she went to her boyfriend, and he gave me the money for me to go.

I felt no shame in taking the money, at least in that moment. But then the more I thought about it, I became angry and confused about the fact the money came from my mom's boyfriend, and so I avoided using the money while in Libya. This would upset my mom since she did not understand it, so eventually, I did buy some things for myself while on the trip to make her happy.

It was after I returned home that I learned our community was not so kind to our family. I discovered our town had judgments of me because of my family life—my mom having a boyfriend was a big no-no. The judgements started with the adults, but then it trickled down to my friends, who started rejecting me due to my mom's actions.

But the adults' behaviors were worse. For example, after I came back from Libya, my math teacher at my school made me stand up by the board so he could shame me. He made fun of my clothes—Levi jeans, an Indian blouse and jewelry. He asked me, "Who is your designer?" I told him, "I am my own designer." He did not like my response. He told me to take off all my jewelry, even though there were other students in the classroom who were wearing jewelry. He then launched all my jewelry out the window. I was embarrassed, and I left the classroom to pick up my belongings. I did not return to the class until the next day, when the teacher told me I was going to fail the class. After that, I did not return to that class until the last day of school.

At the end of the school year, one of my teachers sent me to another room to pick up something they needed. I went, and when I opened the door, I saw the math teacher (the same one who threw my jewelry out the window) passionately kissing the music teacher. I ran out, and he ran after me out of embarrassment and worry. Luckily, I returned to my previous classroom safely.

On the last day of school, I decided to return to that teacher's class. He called my name and said to me, "You passed the class." It was his way of saying "thank you" for not telling anyone what I saw. But he still didn't like me. He said, "You will never amount to anything. I suggest you look to get married as soon as possible."[3]

As for him, he did not marry the music teacher I saw him kissing. It was uncovered after the war that he had a problem with pedophilia.

---

[3] Author's Notes—When adults of authority are in positions they have no business being in, they can be quite dangerous, resulting in children experience trauma from their cruelties. This is why people who as children experience trauma at the hands of adults have trust issues when they become adults themselves.

My First Love: Mirsad

In my adolescence, I was extremely busy. I participated in many organized activities throughout the countryside. It was through my travels that I would meet my first love, Mirsad. He was the son of the communist mayor in town.

My attraction to Mirsad was because he loved me unconditionally. He would walk me home at night and buy me special treats at the bakery. Mirsad was a kind individual and treated me with respect. Even though he knew about my family situation, he was never judgmental about it. Mirsad knew what our peers thought about me, and why most men did not want to have a relationship with me. But he didn't care about what other people thought.

One night, I saw my mom's boyfriend as we were walking home. I sped up and went ahead of Mirsad. He rushed to catch up with me and said, "Are you afraid of him?" I knew at that point, Mirsad knew why I was afraid, and it was like a kick in the gut. I was truly embarrassed. Mirsad was silent, and he just stayed with me. He was the first man to not judge me and love me for who I am.

When I met the mayor, he was just as accepting as Mirsad. At the time, it gave me hope. It was refreshing to meet a family that was kind and accepting. I also learned from this experience that those who judged me were taught to be intolerant of others, but not everyone is taught his way.

For people that are judged by their peers, acceptance and trust from another individual comes with "what ifs." It is hard for someone who is harshly judged their entire life to be accepting of acceptance. Mirsad and his family are a reminder that good people are out there for all of us to discover.

My Second Relationship

Things eventually ended with Mirsad, and I met someone else from another town when I was in high school. My second boyfriend was beloved by my mom. Unfortunately, I cannot remember his name. He served in the army after high school when he was 18 years old, which was mandatory under communist rule. When he came home from service, my mom was quick to tell me that I should get married to this man.

At this point in my life, my mother was constantly missing in action. She would spend days, and sometimes weeks, away from home. She would stay at her boyfriend's apartment and leave me home to deal with my father and brother. I shouldered the burden of cooking and cleaning for the two men in the house, while I wondered why she would do this to me.

The confusion I felt from this time in my life was overwhelming. Taking care of my father and brother caused more resentment and more anger towards my mother. At the time, I felt like my brother was immune to what was going on. Men were more protected from shame and abuse.

Today, I can see that my mother was not a bad person, but I could not understand her actions at this time. My anger and resentment caused me to grieve my mother's life, as it was a life that had been cursed. I would cry because I could not see a future for her. I could not imagine her as a grandmother for my kids. I began to realize that something bad would eventually happen to her. Every night that my mother did not come home, I waited for someone to tell me that she died. I buried my mother mentally and emotionally long before I buried her physically. [4]

----

[4] Author's Note—If you have lived a traumatic life, you will understand Mance's thinking. Many who read this book may have a friend or relative with a cursed life. We may struggle with their actions toward us. As time goes on, a mental shift starts to happen. We prepare ourselves for disappointment and loss.

During this chapter, I thought about my relationship with my own mother. She was an immigrant from Italy. While warm and loving to others, she was not the most loving mom. She could not say "I love you." Her advice was often critical. Her way of loving us was to tell us to "toughen up" or that "life is not easy, wake up son." My mom thought showing love and compassion to her children was a sign of weakness.

I had an epiphany while talking to Mance that my own mother was impacted by violence and dysfunction. I never could account for this growing up. The blessing of understanding trauma is that we all have our own experiences that we must come to terms with. I love my mom with all my heart, and I now understand that as a child, she lived a cursed life too.

Living on the Edge

My mother lived two lives—one for herself and one for her family. Despite this, she still cared about my father. She would come home and ask us, "Did you cook for your father? Is his room warm? How is your dad feeling?" Throughout the separation, my father was the same toward my mother—as long as they lived together under one roof, he wanted to have control over her.

Normally, when my mom came home from her boyfriend's house, she would scratch on the window while my father was asleep, and I would let her in. At times, my mom felt it would be safer if she could sleep with me. My father would sometimes sit waiting for her, not realizing she had already come back and was sleeping my bed. There were other times when my father would wake up and be furious when he found her in bed with me instead of with him.

We both became a target for my father—my mom for her discretions, and me for protecting my mom. Our behaviors offended him, but I found solace in the fact that I saved my mother's life on many occasions.[5]

One night, when my mom came home late from her boyfriend's house, my father was waiting for her while sitting in a chair with a knife. When my mom entered the house and saw my father, she knew the knife was a threat toward her. Her coming home late was the ultimate betrayal.

---

[5] Author's Note—The solace Mance felt from her mother hugging her in bed is a powerful statement about the human condition. When a person is not appropriately loved by a parent, any small form of love from them fills a void in the heart and mind of that individual.

Her boyfriend did not offer her safety either. He was just another male that came in her life and took advantage of her. He would abuse her, same as my father did. The abuse from her boyfriend intensified as their relationship went on. One night, she came home soaking wet from head to toe. I asked her what happened, and my mother told me her boyfriend had been waiting for her by a bridge. They had an argument, and he threw her over the bridge.

The abuse came from an all too familiar place of my mom just wanting to be loved. She could not recognize the insanity of what happened—she was blind to it. She was continually rescued by strangers, like the people who pulled her out of the river that day.

After the fight by the river, I approached my mother's boyfriend and told him, "If I ever see you with my mother again, I will kill you." I then confronted my mom about divorcing my father and ending the relationship with her boyfriend. I told her, "I will never have relationships like this." I felt some guilt for saying this, as the cultural norms of Bosnia were the root cause of why she hadn't divorced my father, but I would learn from watching her that a good divorce is better than a bad marriage.

Counseling and Premonitions

My mom wanted to get help, but psychiatric help in Yugoslavia was a sign of weakness. If you had to go to a psychiatrist, that meant you were crazy. This caused people to deny their issues or find alternate forms of treatment.

My mom sought advice from her boyfriend's sister. Her boyfriend did not like his sister, and he had not even mentioned her existence before. It was an acquaintance who told my mom about the sister and her "gift."

My mom talked to Kada about it, and Kada encouraged her to go see the sister for help. My mom then managed to talk her boyfriend into visiting his sister, explaining that she could get some help for her issues that no one else cared about. The only thing most people cared about was to judge my mom for her cursed life.

My mom told Kada about the visit afterward, saying that it was odd. She travelled to a poor village far away. When they arrived, they discovered that the sister's son was in bed with a high fever. Her boyfriend was estranged from his sister, and after saying hello, he said little else. He acted like he was embarrassed and refused to talk to his nephew. He left without my mother and did not come back for two days.

The woman told my mother, "You are not the wife of my brother." My mom asked, "Do you think I will ever have a life with him?" The sister responded, "I know why you came to visit me." My mom did not understand what that meant.

His sister told my mom, "I will pray tonight and tell you my advice tomorrow." The next day, she told my mother, "Your daughter will be successful, but not here. Your son will be fine. And you will die with your husband, Alija."

The Abandoned Puppy

One day, I found my mother laying on the ground crying. She seemed lost, as if her entire world was coming to an end. Her behavior reminded me of an abandoned puppy. When I asked my mom what happened, she said, "He is going to get married."

My mother's boyfriend, unbeknownst to her, had met another woman, and he was going to marry her. Adding to her shock, the woman was one of my mother's friends. Then, to add another layer of irony, I was friends with the daughter of the woman he was marrying. My friend was upset with this marriage. She felt empathy for my mother, and the grief she was experiencing.

Ultimately, the marriage not last very long. They were together for a short time, and then the woman left him. Within weeks, it was over. However, I am still friends with the daughter. We talk occasionally, including about how dangerous this man had been in our collective lives.

My mom spent many nights crying after her boyfriend left her. I would be trying to sleep and would hear her trying to suffocate the moans. In her mind, she had nothing left to live her. Her pain sounded like death was on the horizon.

She would sit by the window smoking cigarettes, waiting for him to come, even though she knew it was never going to happen. She avoided everyone due to her shame. I tried to give my mom hope. I would make up stories that I saw him, and he was coming back. I felt bad for my mom, and this was the only thing I could think of to help her.

Looking back, I think my mother had a nervous breakdown. She would never fully recuperate from this tragic event. This event was a catalyst for what I feared as the worse outcome. I began to worry about what life would be like without my mother. I was not waiting for her eventual death—she died the evening she found out the man she loved did not love her back.

Married but not Merry

I soon graduated from high school. My mother was troubled by her own loneliness and lack of romantic prospects, and so she pressured me to marry after high school. Since my mom had nothing to look forward to regarding her own future, she thought my getting married would somehow save her.

Looking back, my mom never asked me if I wanted to be married— she would just say to me it would be good for me to be married. I did not want to disappoint her, which led to me succumbing to her wishes and agreeing to get married at the first opportunity. By summer's end, I would find my first husband.

My mom had already identified a future husband, but he would have to wait. I told my mom that before I got married, I wanted the summer to enjoy my time. She agreed and let me travel across Yugoslavia. Leaving for the summer was the right thing to do. I considered it self-care in exchange for giving my life to another man.

As with anyone living a cursed life, complications happened. During my summer tour, I met another man. I was enamored by him. He looked like James Dean. We hit it off, and we became very close. He told me that he loved me and wanted to marry me. I said, "YES!"

I thought "James Dean" was the guy for me. He was not the man that my mom had wanted, but he was much better than her choice. When I told my mom that he was who I wanted to marry, and that I would not marry the man she had chosen, she simply said, "Okay, no problem." My mom probably knew the man she chose was not invested in me, and she just wanted me to be happy.

The fact that I was marrying James Dean upset some people because he was from the village. In Eastern Europe, being from the village meant you were the lowest part of the communist caste system. Houses in the village were primitive and had minimal services, if any at all. For example, James had grown up in a home lacking water and a bathroom

The people most upset with my decision were my father and brother. My mother told me to tell my father about "my" intentions to be married. When I told my father, he agreed to buy me a wedding dress, but didn't say much else. I saw sadness in his eyes. I was confused by his reaction.

James visited my hometown while we were still engaged. By the time he visited, my mother had lost interest in my getting married, and my father had become enraged over it. My father did not like James because he came from a village that resembled a third world country. With both parents having such varied opinions, I decided to elope, just to piss them off.

After visiting my hometown, we visited James' village. Compared to how James was treated in my village, the reaction to my arrival in his village was quite different. We were the talk of the town. James had a small family, and the villagers served as an extended family. The first time they met me, there was a sense of merriment and curiosity. An educated woman from the city marrying an uneducated man from the village was unheard of in the communist caste system. My mother-in-law and new family were so proud of their son's choice—a different reality than what I had experienced from my own parents.

What I realized after writing this chapter was what made the biggest positive impression on me was my future in-laws. It did not matter that they did not have running water and modern amenities, because they had each other. For me, it was important to see a loving relationship.

Cultural Shifts

After we eloped, reality soon kicked me in the ass. We had a short-lived honeymoon period before the rigors of marriage were tested. It was a bit of a culture shock since they lacked all the basic amenities, and I did not how to live without them. I had minimal skills—I could not start the wooden stove, nor did I know how to complete daily routines like outdoor laundry and cooking, which took place in all weather conditions. If the water froze, my father-in-law would break the ice with an axe. My mother-in-law would not allow me to ask my husband for help since he was the boss.

My new family was very patient with me at first, but they expected I would become the dutiful wife that was customary in Yugoslavia. My mother-in-law wanted me traditional in my clothing and appearance, like cutting my nails, avoiding nail polish, and giving up makeup. I could not cut or color my hair, and I had to be covered from head to toe. This was mandatory in the village.

Everything I had learned from my mother had to be discarded for me to be successful in my new marriage. But this new lifestyle did not bother me since everyone was nice to me. I did not mind subscribing to the cultural changes, with one exception. There was a tension between Bosnian Muslims and Serbian Christians, which was an omen of the impending conflict that would engulf all of Yugoslavia. My family was connected to Serbs by marriage. On my mom's side of the family, my aunt and uncle were married to Catholics and Christians. Because of this, my mother-in-law was adamant they could not come visit me, which felt like a shot to the head for me.

Gossip about mom's history traveled to the village. My mother-in-law started asking me about my mom's former lover. Her questions would add more intrigue, as the person that my mom's boyfriend decided to marry was related to my mother-in-law's family. My mother-in-law had strong opinions of my mom's former boyfriend.

The multiple struggles I went through at this time fed into each other. My lack of domestic skills, combined with my inability to navigate cultural norms that were different than my personal upbringing, caused old wounds with my parents to resurface. I was angry at how ill-prepared I was. All of this created a vulnerability in my new marriage that I was not ready to confront.

The Lies of Marriage

Things in our house were strange. There was always a commotion in the house, but when I opened the door, it would grow quiet. I found some solace in my father-in-law—he was kind to me, and honest. One day, my father-in-law was chopping wood for winter. I went out to help him, and while he chopped, he told me to sit. He then said, "My son lied to you." He told me that his son did not work and was uneducated—he had only a middle school education.

My father in-law was frustrated, and I could see it in in his face. He worked hard to provide for his family, but he was the only one and the sole provider. My father-in-law was worried that there would always be a lack of help, and it would always fall on him to keep the family together.

I became pregnant after six months of marriage. Around the same time, I learned my parents were cutting me off. They did not want anything to do with my current situation. I was left alone to contemplate what I should do next with my life.

Medically, my dental health was suffering, as I had an infected tooth. The only cure the villagers could provide was tea based on folklore cures. The pain was getting worse, so finally my father-in-law and I walked to the dentist in the city, since we did not have the money for a bus. We had to walk through woods and back roads for three hours to get there.

When I saw the dentist, I had to have my tooth pulled, but because I didn't have insurance, it was without Novocain. I screamed when it was pulled out. The dentist[6] did not charge me because he felt so bad. He knew me when I was beautiful

---

[6] Author's Note— During the war, the dentist was shot and killed by the Chetnik soldiers.

young lady—his wife was my elementary school teacher. He was shocked by the turn of events in my life. I imagine being in the dentist's shoes and seeing an old man bring me in—a pregnant woman from a remote village.

My husband did not come with me that day. It was too much of an embarrassment for him. While leaving the hospital, I ran into my father, as he worked across the street. He was embarrassed by my appearance, so he crossed the street and did not acknowledge me. He turned his back to me until my father-in-law and I left town.

Men in my life have a pattern of letting me down but my father-in-law was an exception. He accompanied me the rest of the way home. When he saw my father turn the other way, he comforted me. He was stunned that my own father would shun me after such a painful experience.

Reconnecting

I started to feel like a slave in my own home. I served everyone, and I grew tired of laboring for free for my new family, like when my sister-in-law would leave her children with me for extended periods of time. I had become tired of it, and I told them I had enough.

I let my husband know I wanted to visit my mother and father. When we went to visit my parents, I wore my wedding dress, since I had nothing else to wear. At my parents' house, my mother hid from me, pretending that she was not home. When I went to gather my personal belongings, I discovered all my possessions were gone. The empty house made me realize my mother had given up on me.

My husband and I walked three hours back to the village. I remember it vividly. I was sad that all memories of my childhood were gone with all my belongings. I was suffering the loss of my family. I was hungry and thirsty, and I was still pregnant. All my husband cared about, though, was being intimate with me in the woods. He was so angry that I refused to be intimate with him, he practically forced himself on me, and almost raped me.

When I arrived home, my mother-in-law opened the door and said, "Your mother did not want to see you?" She immediately knew what had happened, and she enjoyed it. I was helpless, and she found pleasure in knowing that.

Months later, a woman in the village brought a message from my mom that stated, "You can come and visit." I went again in my wedding dress. This time, my mom opened the door, and she hugged and kissed me. I was kind of numb, but I could see that my mom was heartbroken. It was an eye-opener.

My father finally talked to me. I asked him why he ignored me when he saw me after my dental appointment. He said, "I was so hurt when I saw the condition of you and your father-in-law." He also mentioned my husband's appearance when we had visited before, saying, "You were wearing old clothes I bought for you, and your husband had tired, worn-out clothing and shoes." My father had wondered what happened to me. He wanted his daughter back, the one that danced across Yugoslavia. He was upset that I exchanged the life I use to have for one of a peasant.

My parents offered to pay our rent and support us so that we could move to Sarajevo. However, as the months went by, my parents became tired of my husband not working. They stopped paying our rent. My husband said he would start working, and I believed him.

When came time to pay our rent, we instead went to visit his parents in the village. I discovered he was manipulating me and lying about having a job—he had only been pretending to go to work. My in-laws knew he did not have job, but they did not have a problem with him lying to me. He was their son, and no matter what, they would give him a pass. We ended up losing the apartment in Sarajevo, and we went back to the village with our tails between our legs. My life of obedience to my in-laws returned.

A Life Begins, A Life Ends

My mother's love was strong—she had changed and was now more nurturing. When it came time for me to give birth, she requested I move back home to do so. She said that my husband could visit, but he could not stay there due to his lies, and her wanting to take care of me without his interference.

When I went home, I also learned how much my father loved me. One day, while I was cleaning his room, I found my picture in his nightstand. I did not understand at the time that even though he was a wounded soul, he still loved his daughter. I was elated to find the picture since I realized he loved me. I hadn't yet forgiven for the abuse he caused when I was a child, but finding that picture brought some peace for me.

After I moved back in with my parents, my husband's cousin would visit often, but in my dad's mind, it was too often. My dad hated my husband's cousin. The cousin was a complicated man that killed many people as a solider during World War II. He would brag how easy it was. My father's frustrations with him grew over time, and it came to a breaking point shortly after I gave birth.

When I had my child, my husband never came to the hospital to visit me, nor did my in-laws. My roommate in the hospital had a visit from her husband. He kissed her feet and lovingly thanked her for having a son. I did not know the joy of a loving and supportive husband like she did. My father was happy to have a grandchild, but distant toward my son and me. My mother was the only person who shared in my joy.

One night in January, my mom gave my son a bath, then said she was going out to visit a friend whose mother died. She never returned home.

I was restless that night and woke up early in the morning, having heard something hit the window. As I was sitting in the living room, I noticed people were looking in our windows. I wondered what was happening, and my gut said something was wrong.

My father returned home from work crying. He told me that my mom was dead. He said that she had been killed by my husband's cousin. My mother had been found dead in his car, shot at close range. No one knew how she ended up there—did he stop her, force her in the car? I would never find out.

My husband's cousin killed himself after my mother was murdered. He shot himself in the middle of downtown, in front of a mosque. No one knows why he did it in public. People started to talk that he was my mother's lover, but I knew this was not true. He was a villager who somehow lived downtown and has not a respected man. He was not a person whom my mom would find attractive. Unfortunately, my mom's past fueled the malicious gossip.

The death of my mom caused an epiphany for my father. He realized that he loved my mother, and he felt guilty about her death. Through this experience, my father learned how to grieve. He would cry and struggle from the guilt regarding their relationship. This would lead to a change in our relationship, and I forgave my father. When it came to my mom herself, however, I felt numb. I could not cry for my mom's death.

My mother's death was unfortunately painful gossip spread by many people. In fact, part of my town celebrated my mother's death. One night, my husband went out for some drinks. He went bar to bar, hearing how people disparaged my mother. When he came home, we had an argument. He was drunk and said, "Nobody says anything nice about your mother."

I can understand how some people can be vicious after someone dies. And while I don't think my husband was a bad person, him participating in the comments and gossip was beyond what I could tolerate. A part of me died because of his cruel response to my mother's death. Even today, I resent the fact that he was my husband. If you really love someone, you support them, instead of allowing the gossip to come into your home. While I have forgiven for his comments, there are some events in a person's life that you cannot forget.

Medical Traumas

One day at while I was at work, I noticed people in the lunchroom whispering to each other. I knew somehow the whispers had to do with me. Finally, a woman came over to me and said, "Do you know what happened to your brother?" She told me that he had a machine accident at his job that cut off his right hand.

I rushed home to find my father in shock. It was confusing for him. A week earlier, my brother had hit my father with the hand he had just lost. I could not tell how my father was feeling, but he appeared to be emotionally hurt. It was painful to watch my father in this condition. I knew I needed to hold it together for my father since I was his world. Knowing I had the ability to be strong for my father was meaningful.

The accident occurred during the 1984 Winter Olympics in Sarajevo. I would visit my brother in the hospital while Olympians were competing nearby. My brother had to have an eight-and-a-half-hour surgery to remove what was left of his hand. The woman who performed the operation acted like it was a simple procedure and not a big deal to lose a hand. My brother was not bothered by her behavior, but it truly irritated me.

A couple of days later, my brother needed another surgery due to thrombosis, which meant losing more of his hand. No matter what errors were made by the doctors, he would never become angry with them. But with me, he would repeatedly hit me for no reason. In our culture, people like doctors were given a pass for life-threatening actions, but that same compassion was not given to female family members for far less serious infractions.

My brother initially a good attitude about losing his hand, mostly because he thought he was going to get a big settlement. However, due to the rules of communism, the workplace accident was covered up, and did not get the large settlement he wanted. The girl at the factory he was teaching at the time of the accident was given a promotion, which added insult to injury.

A few weeks after my brother's accident, while I was eating dinner with my father, our family would suffer another serious medical event. My father dropped at the sink. His mouth drooped, and he was showing signs of having a stroke. I rushed him to the hospital, where they confirmed that he indeed had suffered a stroke.

I had the neighbors watch my son while I nursed my brother and father during their time of need. They would both recuperate over time, but the stroke left my father in terrible shape. He was a quadriplegic and could not walk nor toilet himself. I had to help rehabilitate him. It would take a year or so before he regained independence.

My brother recuperated too after staying in the hospital for a long time. When he got out, he started to travel more. He was very depressed, and his character would darken. But like our mother, there was no help to be found for him. Asking for help was still an embarrassment in our society. Between my father's physical invalidity and my brother's emotional invalidity, I had to become the caretaker for the two men in my life, and continued to live at home to support them.

Trouble at Work

I was still trying to keep my marriage together. Despite huge tensions between my brother, father, and husband, normalcy was starting to return to my life. My husband had started to work, and we decided to get an apartment.

I started to work at the company where my mom used to work. I had an economics degree, but I was given a housekeeping job. The director of the company had been my economics teacher in school, and he promised me a better job in the future.

One night, the director had a party in his office, which was more like a large conference room. I was tasked with serving alcohol at the party. At the end of the night, after everyone else had left, I helped the director clean up the office. When I went to leave, I found the door to the office had been locked. I could smell the alcohol on my boss's breath as he approached behind me.

I pushed him away. He told me, "What do you think you are doing? Who was your mother?" I pushed him away again and grabbed a trophy to strike him. I told him I would not sleep with a chauvinistic, disgusting human being, and told him to unlock the door. He let me out. I went home, where I had a restless night, unable to sleep.

I did not know how spiteful he would become after I rejected his advances. The next morning, he drove his car through a pothole near where I was walking, just to splash the dirty water all over me. His friends starting calling me, wanting to know if it was true that I slept with him, and that they would rape me if I lied about it. Two weeks later, I was fired.

When I told my husband about being fired, he was indifferent. I started to look for another job while my mental health continued to decline. I would dream of the demise of my boss after he fired me. He has since died from cancer, but if he was around today, I would have liked to confront him about what he did to me[7].

---

[7] Author's Note— When a person dies before someone can share how their actions caused them trauma, it's a lost opportunity for the hurt person to reconcile their trauma. To this day, Mance gets a knot in her stomach when she talks about her former boss.

A Good Divorce is Better Than a Bad Marriage

I took a job at a motel restaurant to pay rent. My mother-in-law took in my son since Yugoslavia did not have any options for childcare. The shift had later hours, so I would come home at 2am. The late nights would lead to speculation by the locals. People suspected I was promiscuous, just like my mother. But we were broke, and I had to work.

My husband and I struggled during this time. After I paid the bills, we had nothing left for food, nor did I have any money to visit my son at my in-laws' house. I was trying to save us, but it seemed like I was the only one.

My father and brother were upset with me. They felt that I had a husband, and he should be a part of the solution. I soon discovered that it was even more than that—my husband wasn't a part of the solution because he was actively contributing to our money problems. Without me realizing it, some of my paycheck had been going to my husband's drinking tab in the same motel where I worked. The owner of the motel made me aware of this one night.

I also learned that, for the second time, my husband had only been pretending to go to work. He had been fired from his job some time ago and not told me. When he woke up in the morning, he went through the motions of acting like he was going to work. After I left the house, he would return home. I had to learn from our landlord that he had been fired.

When I confronted him, he raised his hands like a doctor and said, "Look at my hands. These are doctor's hands." I replied, "Look at my hands, swollen from work at home and at my job. I do everything!" He told he was going to visit his parents. I told him, "Bring me back my child."

I went to talk to my father, which was the best decision I could have made. When I explained my situation, he said to me, "I am not going to push or tell you what to do, but I am not going to pay rent for this situation. Instead, you can come back to my house and stay here rent-free with your child." I realized that I had no more love for my husband, only pain and suffering.

My father also said, "You have to quit that job due to its crazy hours. It is not okay." He based his advice on communist perceptions since people working in hospitality were at the lower end of the communist caste system.

The next day, I cleaned out the apartment. I left one sleeping bag, a clock, and some clothes that belonged to my husband. I will never forget how it felt to do this. When my husband came to the apartment and discovered I was gone, he went to my father's house to bring me my child.

My father was sitting in the backyard. I told my father that my husband was going to sleep overnight so we can talk about things. My father said to my husband, "How about you help me with the garden and cleaning?" My husband said, "I am not here to do your garden for you, you crippled man. Get off your own crippled ass and clean your own yard." I overheard this and froze. My father had tried to be a good person, giving my husband clothing, food, and a roof over his head, and this was how my husband decided to repay him.

I asked my husband to come in the house, then I grabbed him and put him up against the door. I said to him, "You bastard! You are under my father's roof. Get the fuck out of my life!" My father's tears had finally provided the inspiration for me to send my husband packing. I then promised myself that I would never let another human being hurt me and my family again.

My father told me that he would give me his pension to pay for a lawyer. He turned everything over to me, and he reassured me that a good divorce is better than a bad marriage. He supported me, which was redemption for his past mistakes. His daughter had been hurt, but no one was going to hurt her anymore. He had changed for the better.

My husband did not want a divorce, but I went forward with it anyhow. Due to my stability, the courts gave me full custody of my son. Unfortunately, my now ex-husband threatened me and tried to steal my son from the front yard. He would never change. He still wouldn't find a job, nor did he fight very hard to visit his son.

I continued to stay with my father, who threw me a divorce party. He was so happy, he invited everyone. Friends and neighbors joined in the celebration. It was very memorable.

My Brother's Resentment

Everything of my father's went to me, including his income. I took care of everything, which my brother resented. After our mother's death, he distanced himself from me and our father, even though we all lived in the same house. He would assume an attitude toward us that was like how our father had acted with our mom[8].

My brother was very medically fragile from developing Hepatitis C as a child. He would never marry or have kids, maybe due to our upbringing and experiences. But he was highly intelligent. He was an alchemist, and he liked the forests and scouting. He had worked in a furniture factory and was a great mechanic. But he would slowly become our father at his worst.

My brother started to treat me like my father had treated me and our mother. He became abusive towards me. Sometimes, I would see myself as my mother, and I would see my brother as my father, doomed to repeat the past and powerful trauma we experienced as kids.

One day, I was teaching my child how to use a spoon. Something I did caused a reaction from my brother, and he punched and slapped me so hard, I lost an earring. I looked in the mirror and saw the imprint of five fingers on my face. My brother said, "I am now God, and I put you in order." He tried to imply I was under his control.

My father saw what happened. We talked, and he said to me, "If I die, do not live with your brother. You need to find

---

[8] Author's Note—This chapter is a great example of parental impact. Mance's brother subconsciously followed in his father's footsteps, as can be common for men to do.

someone who is educated and eventually get married." He was telling me not to make the same mistakes I made before. My father was, for the first time, understanding the role of fatherhood.

That slap was such a powerful experience, I told myself that this would be the last time my brother, or any man, was going to hit me. The next day, my brother came into the room like nothing ever happened. I grabbed a vase and hit him with it. I said, "How are you feeling? That was the last time you will hit me. Next time, I will kill you." I wanted him to feel the same pain he caused me.

I question to this day, why did I have to do this to show him that he was doing was wrong? Why did I have to hit him to get him to stop hitting me?

Fixing The Past

I started to rekindle healthy relationships with my friends, meeting them in coffee bars. I also started running as a hobby. I would jog kilometers at a time to help cope with the pain. I began to mature and become a beautiful woman, even though I still had the bell around my neck from my mother's indiscretions, which was common knowledge in the village. Still, I found myself.

My brother was not so fortunate. He could not shake off the toxicity of the past. I had put a stop to his physical abuse, but the mental and emotional abuse continued. When I would come home late at night, he would lock the door. He would call me a bitch and started to wait for me like our father did with our mother.

One day, I had enough, and I went to the shed and grabbed a wooden handle. I started to smash every window in the house. I said, "Every window in this house is now a door for me. You are not my husband or my father. You do this one more time, you will have this handle strike your back."

Another afternoon, my brother used lots of hot water in the bathtub. In Yugoslavia, the boiler had to warm the water, which could get expensive. My father became upset about the amount of hot water that my brother used. My brother started to fight with our father and hit him, and I had to step in for protection. I grabbed a frying pan and hit my brother, which made him stop hitting our father.

I realize now that my brother learned to resort to physical violence from our father, and I defended my father similar to how I learned to protect my mother. Things that are broken in childhood are not easily repaired when we are adults, especially when we don't realize how we have been broken. But by standing up to my brother, I was able to fix one part of my life.

Single Parenting, and a New Marriage

Women in Yugoslavia felt the pressures of single parenting, and in a communist nation, being single with a child comes with stigma. Single women with children were on the lowest rung of the caste system since being single is always the woman's fault, even when they have been abused, slandered and attacked. But if a man is single, no judgement is passed on them. It is never a man's fault.

I grew resentful of my life while I was a single mother. Every day after work, I was expected to be the main caretaker. I was tired of coming home to three males that relied on me for everything.

But all was not lost, even in Yugoslavia. One day, I was walking with my son along the path for bikers and walkers by Rockinitza River. My son picked flowers for me and was acting like a typical boy, throwing stones and having fun. We went to the basketball courts and watched a local team play basketball. I met a man while on our walk, and we started dating.

His name was Elvedin Cuplov, nicknamed "Cuni" (pronounced "soon-e") because he was so tan. He was an accomplished musician and studied geography. He travelled a lot across Europe as part of a successful band. He had built his own home, but we did not live together while we were dating.

My father and brother liked Elvedin. Elvedin came to our house with bouquets of flowers and other goodies that my father enjoyed. He was smart and knew how to befriend my father with gifts. I wanted my dad's approval—I wanted him to be happy and proud of my choice. In a sense, I wanted to make up for my past divorce.

After three years or so of dating, Elvedin asked me to marry him. I told him he had to ask my father. So Elvedin came to our house one day and asked my father for my hand in marriage. My father replied, "Look at me—Mance is a very good daughter. She is very smart, clean, and organized. You will never find another woman like her." He told Elvedin that he will have to take good care of me. I listened in the other room, and thought to myself, "Who does that? Is that my father talking about me?" I could not believe it.

With my dad's blessing, we married in February 1991. Seven months later, I became pregnant with my second child.

Hell Comes to Bosnia

We did not have much time to enjoy our marriage. The political situation in Yugoslavia started to come to a boil to the point where you could feel the hate amongst the different religious groups. Without communist Russia to control the religious turmoil, Serbs were free to engage in genocide. The Serbs increased security and monitoring, establishing check points across the country. Muslims and Roman Catholics were separated out and rounded up for extermination. From Kosovo to Albania, the atrocities started to take a toll.

Television reports covered the genocides that were occurring, and mercenaries were brought in to help the Serbs. We were advised to leave our houses, but my husband refused to leave the home he built with his own hands. Some of his family chose differently and left for Germany.

My brother called one day and said, "Come home and take care of father. I am retreating to the woods so they cannot kill me." I was pregnant at the time. I told my husband to stay in his hometown, and that I would pick up my father and son and bring them back. My husband said, "No, no, I will go with you to protect you." I tried to get my mother-in-law to stop him from coming with me, but he would not listen to any of us.

On the way back to my husband's hometown, with my father and son in tow, we discovered a new checkpoint had been created, and we could not go back. We were stuck with remaining at my father's house in Rogatica.

My husband's brothers called and told us to stay in Rogatica because war was starting in my husband's hometown. We could hear the rifles in the background on the phone. My in-laws were sent to stay with us in Rogatica for safety, but at the checkpoint, the Serbs only let my mother-in-law through. My father-in-law had to go back.

Amid all this, I discovered my husband had developed a serious problem with alcohol and would drink excessively while living with me and our family. I tried to reason with him to stop drinking, but with little success. I did not understand it at the time, but in hindsight, I understand it was due to the uncertainty of our situation. He had major anxiety attacks worrying about me and his mother, and alcohol was a way to soothe his troubles.

The stress from everything was impacting my pregnancy and getting worse by the day. Along with the war, I had to cook for everyone, take care of my father, and live without any electricity. We started to hear grenades outside of town as the Serbs moved to occupy the area. We began sleeping at our neighbor's house since their house was made of concrete, which was safer from grenade launches.

Lines and lines of people were leaving, each saying to us, "Get out, they are killing everyone!" But my husband would not leave, even though my mother-in-law kept asking him to go. Our neighbors were in denial too, believing the Serbs would not kill us.

As things fell apart, I overheard a conversation between my mother-in-law and husband. She said to him, "If you stay living with her, I will never talk to you again in my life. She is only worried about her father. We need to get out of here now." She wanted him to divorce me.[9]

---

[9] Author's Note—Mance struggled with sharing this passage, but I felt it important to include as a story about pain and forgiveness, which is a part of healing. The experiences of a holocaust are real and

My son in my womb gave me a sharp pain as I heard this. When I confronted my husband about what I overheard, he said, "I have to listen to my mother. We are going to leave this country when this war is over." He asked me to look at him, and he said, "Even when I am 80 years old, I want you to sleep in my arms." This would be among his last words.

He went on patrol that evening. I told Elvedin not to drink while out, but he came back home drunk anyhow. He could hardly talk. That night, I had a dream that my husband lost all his teeth from the local mercenaries. Time had run out for us, and now it was too late to escape.

---

unexplainable, as are how people react to being frightened for their lives. Mance does not hold on to any anger over what her mother-in-law said. She understands the context of why Elvedin's mother would want him to leave. She was his mother, and her natural instinct was to protect her son, just as it was for Mance to protect her son from harm.

Black Friday

The following is an account from Mance's testimony to the War Tribunal. On occasion, initials are used in the following chapters to protect the anonymity of others.

On Friday, June 19th, 1992, we became locked in. We watched in the morning as the circle of Serbs around our town closed in on us. Our home was totally cutoff from the rest of the city. We could not escape the horrors. Little did I know at the time, everything I had known would soon disappear in flames, and some of our neighbors would become murderers.

Around noon, I saw the Serbian mercenaries with their black masks come in and start the ethnic cleansing in our town. They lined up on both sides of the street and started entering the homes. I prepared a wheelbarrow for my father so I could push him. My father said, "They are not going to kill me. I will hide in the basement." I had bathed my father the night before, so I left him some food in the basement as the rest of us prepared to escape.

I saw the mercenaries come into my father's yard. I carried my son as I tried to jump over the neighbor's fence. My husband helped his mother out. I made it to another street when I heard screaming and yelling. I turned around and saw my father's home in flames.

Everything was dark, and it started to rain. It sounded like tears. In the background, a Serbian tank played music, celebrating as my father was burned alive. The same fate was met by my neighbors. Everything was in flames. Whatever they could burn, they did. Whatever they could kill, they did.

For whatever reason, some of the neighbors wound up in the house of Murisa Garagica, including my husband Elvedin, my son Senko, and my mother-in-law Lelja. When we arrived in the house, I saw Hazim Skaljic, his wife Aida, and their two children, who were both under a year old. I also remember the Hurmovic family was there. They had two kids as well. These two families will forever be in my hearts and mind.

My neighbor Ramiz Alic was also there with his three sisters: Rasema, Ramiza, and Fikreta. Ramiz was a large man, and the sisters tried to hide him in comforters and blankets. Ramiz was the uncle of the Hurmovic family, and he had a problem with one of his neighbors, Boben Pericic. Prior to the conflict, they disputed over their land. Neighborhood arguments that would otherwise be typical turned divisive during the war. Before the war, Boben would tell Ramiz "I will kill you1" when they argued. His threat would come true thanks to the ethnic cleansing.

Everyone thought the house was a safe place to hide until the bullets and grenades started. Our street was blocked while the Serbs cleansed the neighborhood, and our area was next. The bullets set the house on fire, which was intentional on the part of the mercenaries. The mercenaries knew we were in there and allowed it to burn.

Everyone started to panic. My husband tried to break a window, and I remember the homeowner saying, "Don't break the window." My husband said, "I will replace the window after the war." My husband threw my son out the window. I jumped out the window after him and landed in front of a mercenary. All I saw was bloodshot eyes behind a mask. He hit me hard with the back of his gun on the back of my head. He said, "What are you doing, you Muslim bitch? You are carrying a dog." He grabbed my son and slammed him against the side of the house so hard, my son's braces popped off, and he started bleeding.

While I was getting beat up, my husband grabbed my son and pulled him back in through the window. After my beating, I too went back into the burning house. The only people left in the house now were Hazim, his wife and children, and my husband and son.

I remember that my neighbor grabbed his little baby girl, holding her close and walking with his wife and son behind him. He declared that we all had to get out, since he thought it was safe to do so. We headed for the door. When Hazim approached the porch, the mercenaries yelled, "Put the child down!"

We saw two lines of mercenaries had formed—one for hitting people in the back of the head with the guns, and one for catching the victims as they fell from the beatings. As the mercenaries beat Hazim, his wife snuck behind him and grabbed the baby.

A Chetnik mercenary hit my husband in the front of his head, and I saw blood trickling down his face from where he was struck on. Another mercenary hit him in the back of the head. They resumed beating me up too. I tried to run in between them to minimize the beating. I tried to push my son in front of me so my body could serve as a shield for him from these unimaginable brutal acts of violence.

A group of us ended up on Tekija street. Hazim's clothes were all bloodstained. In the middle of the street, lying down in a pool of blood, was Ramiz Alic. Boben Pericic was behaving like a mass murderer, tearing Ramiz apart for all to witness, yelling, "Where is your motherfucking shotgun now?!"

The three sisters fell on top of Ramiz as shields, begging Boben to stop. They were yelling, "Please do not kill the only brother we have!" Boben showed no mercy, beating up the sisters so he could get back to torturing Ramiz.

In all this madness, we were frozen by horror. The sisters were pulled off their brother, and we were commanded to stand facing the wall of the house. We knew this meant we were going to be killed. I placed my son in front of me and started praying to God. I prayed my body would protect my son and the baby inside of me from harm.

A mercenary yelled, "Separate the women and kids from the men! They can go to the concentration camps." Boben screamed, "No, we are going to kill them all!" But he was overruled. The mercenaries started to separate us. There were intense screams of terror as we were ripped from the wall and divided across the street from each other, while Ramiz was still lying in a pool of blood in the middle of the street.

I saw Boben Pericic raise his machine gun and kill all the men. My husband raised his arms to reach out to me. I felt my baby turn inside me as I watched him perish. I would eventually name our child after him as remembrance to him.

I thought to myself, I must fight to live. The women were gathered and told to head towards the church. I was the first one to start running there. Chetniks were holed up in the apartment buildings, firing at us as we ran. I used the burning houses as cover to avoid gunfire. Low to the ground with my son, I lost my mother-in-law in the chaos of it all, but she survived by hiding in a house. She is still alive today.

In the street, Boben Pericic was still beating up Ramiz. One of Ramiz's sisters started to walk towards the Chetniks like a zombie, almost hypnotized. She was headed toward her house, where the men had been lined up and killed. She was searching for her husband.

I thought about calling out to her to save her from harm. She went to Boben and stood in front of him. He yelled, "Where are you going, bitch?!" Boben pulled out his gun and shot her. She dropped to the ground, joining her husband in death.

It started to rain again, and we were all ordered to lay down in the street. A transporter came by playing music that gleefully warned us about our impending rape and death. The lyrics went, *"Bula trobula troje gace obula a caepvrte neca jer catnik sece,"* which translates to, "You can wear three underwear, as by the fourth underwear, you will be dead." The mercenaries shouted, "Today is Black Friday, you bitches!" This term was significant to us as Muslims. Muslim men would normally be in mosque or church on Friday, as Friday is a Muslim day of worship.

The Serbs thought it would be amusing to throw ash trays, bottles, and trash out the windows at the wounded animals in the streets. For over an hour, we lay still and listened to the loud music and Serbian chants. We thought our fate would be the transporter running us over in the streets. After an hour, a young Serbian came and instructed us to move to the old priest's house across the street. We followed in silence until we arrived at the house and went in, where we spent the night, and many nights to follow.

The Next Day

All night, I slept on a rotted floor, along with 30 other women and children in a 3x3 meter room. It had a filthy, wooden floor, like a barn. Some of the mothers, including myself, squatted all night. In the middle of June, fear had brought chills to our village. There were some blankets in the old house. We covered ourselves with them for protection more than warmth. I tried to cover my son with a sweater I had worn around my waist.

When I woke in the early morning, I felt so much pain in my stomach, back, neck, and hips. I looked around me and saw little kids sleeping and hugging their mothers. We resembled bags of dirty laundry. It was warm and muggy the night before, and our body odor was filling up the unventilated room. We were choking on our own smell, but we were too afraid to open a window. We behaved like wounded animals, fearing our mercenary hunters.

We did not have a bathroom. Going 24 hours without a bathroom was causing a burning sensation in my genitals. Another woman had diarrhea, and she used a plastic bag to relieve herself. People cursed at her out of frustration. After using it, she got up and stated she was going to ask a guard to throw away the bag. I let her know I had to go to the bathroom, so we could go together to speak to the guard. I tried to put my sneakers on, but my feet are so swollen, my shoes felt foreign to me and did not fit.

We bravely entered another room of women and children that was without guards. The air was cooler there. The mothers in the room were holding their kids in a protective manner. They looked like wounded animals protecting their herd.

I saw Ramiz's wife sitting on a wooden board on the floor. She had been shot in the leg. She had a huge black eye, and her face was bruised, most likely from being struck by the back of a gun. A Catholic lady named Stipinca sat by the door asleep. On the other side of the door was Hazim's wife. Both women, like Ramiz's wife, were bruised from severe beatings.

A high school girlfriend was there and whispered to me that our friend, J.N., had told her that another friend, R.S., was taken to another building that the Chetniks were using for their command and returned later. I told her to be quiet and let everyone sleep.

The woman with the plastic bag asked me, "Are you coming?" We both knew one knock on the door to where the guards were could end our lives. Simple actions now became complicated.

The doors opened after a few minutes of knocking. I made sure I looked crippled and unappealing. The Chetnik that opened the door said, "Good morning, sister." He was among several men that were very drunk. I asked if we could go to the bathroom. He said, "Of course. Who said you cannot go to the bathroom?" He offered me a bottle of cognac and said, "Drink!" I took a sip, and he instructed us that the bathrooms are behind the house.

When we opened the door, the bathrooms were floating with feces. And here I was in my sneakers that I had flattened to resemble flip flops so that they would fit. I looked around and found a crate. I stepped on the crate and squatted. My urine was full of blood. I did my business while the mercenaries could see my back end. While going to the bathroom, I thought about how the Serbs cared more about their shit than they did us.

I pulled myself together and returned to the house. When I got back, the Chetnik said, "Sister, have a smoke." He gave me a cigarette and lit it for me. I had never smoked before, but I obeyed him and smoked to preserve my life. As I smoked, I smelled pancakes. The priest next door was making pancakes for his wife[10]. He was a prisoner too, though, and could not send us food.

The guard said, "You know what, sister? We stayed up all night to protect you." He then started to blame everything that was happening on the Croatian president. I privately thought, "You are protecting me from who? You piece of shit. You feel so important." I visualized grabbing his throat and killing him. My child was flipping inside of me, reacting to my stress.

My shoes were filled with feces, and I asked if I could go wash them. He said, "No problem, sister, go ahead." He insisted I should have more cognac when I got back. I went outside to wash my sneakers and saw little kids come out of the house. They went to the bathroom and washed their faces. They looked like zombies, not children, due to looking so ill. The mercenaries gave one little boy a bomb to play with to keep him busy. The lack of humanity toward us included our children.

I returned to the house, and we were soon given some food. My mother-in-law had managed to bring her sedatives with her. I asked her for one for me, but I discreetly gave it to my son instead. The Chetniks were picking women like fruit and taking them into the next building to be beaten and raped, and I did not want my son to hear the screams.

I saw a high school girlfriend return from that building next door. Her mother made a space for her to go to sleep. No one spoke to her or asked any questions—we knew what happened to her. She came back with black eyes, and a blank stare. Her black eyes were beyond what most people can picture—they

---

[10] Author's Note—Mance could smell the pancakes as we wrote this chapter. Our senses remember trauma and can bring back dark memories.

carried the mark of both blunt force and emotional trauma. Humanity did not exist in this world. Hope was no longer a part our lives. We lived in hell.

Humanity and Inhumanity

Time as we knew it was gone—dates and times of day no longer existed. With each sunrise, we sweated and smelled worse. Whatever sense of humanity we could keep alive in ourselves, we tried our best. A four-month-old baby, the son of Dr. Mehic, was with us in the church. The baby's mother cried because she lacked sustenance and water, and she could not feed her child. Another mother who was breastfeeding her own child offered to breastfeed the four-month-old, named Allen. He is still alive today, and his mother is now a lawyer.

To illustrate the complications of this region, Dr. Mehic was a Bosnian Muslim. He was best friends with Dr. Radomir, a Bosnian Serbian. They were such good friends, they were best men for each other's weddings. When the mercenaries arrived, Dr. Radomir tried to save Dr. Mehic by letting Dr. Radomir's family hide in his house.

The night we were walked into the priest's house, the mercenaries also brought Dr. Mehic, his wife, and his baby into our house of hell. We questioned Dr. Mehic why Dr. Radomir could not protect him. He told us the mercenaries had found out his family was in hiding at Dr. Radomir's house. Dr. Radomir protested the intrusion and tried to save his friend. He was told by the mercenaries if he did not give up Dr. Mehic, he would die. Dr. Radomir witnessed the brutal beating of his friend in his own home prior to them taking Dr. Mehic and his family to the church.

One night, our captors barged through the door along with my former neighbor, S.L. He was president of the Serbian Party (SDS) and brought a bag of food for all of us to feed the children. His daughter's babysitter, A.H., who was in the house with us, took the bag and put the food on the floor to distribute to everyone in the room.

We lived in a space and time that was void of human decency, and we could not trust anyone trying to help us. We did not know what S.L.'s aim was in coming to us. We wondered if he came to help A.H. due to their personal relationship and was not there for the rest of us. How could we trust this man or think he was being sincere?

S.L. apologized to everyone in the room and said, "I wish I could have done more to save the neighbors." He then let us know he was very busy planning a funeral for his nephew, who was killed after taking part in the cleansing of a close village. How dark of a world, when in one sentence he said he was sorry for not helping save others, and then shared how his nephew died carrying out the ethnic cleansing in another village.

S.L. had been my coworker—I cleaned his office. After my mother died, he had placed a horse penis on his desk, implying she was a whore. I stared at the man who was cruel to me many years prior, telling a story about his nephew dying, and wanting to be considered a hero for helping others. I wished it was him that died instead.

One of the women shared with S.L. that some women were being taken to the other building to be beaten and raped. S.L. took a piece of paper to give to A.H. and wrote, "Do not take or touch this woman or her kids. Signed, S.L. (SDS party)."

While the door was open, some of us went outside. The mother of the four-month-old saw the priest's wife and asked her for some hot water to make formula for her baby. The priest's wife brought her water along with a full pot of pancakes, potatoes, and goulash for all of us. Hidden in the shadows of darkness was hope, given to us by the priest and his wife. It was very brave of her to walk past the mercenaries, risking her life to give us food.

The women started to attack the food, leaving me nothing to eat. One act of humanity can inadvertently bring out inhumanity in others. I cried so hard that I didn't feel hungry anymore. This would be the first time I wished I was dead.

Guardian Angels

In the darkness, I learned that our children saved us. They were guardian angels. If it was not for them, we would not be alive. Instinctually, it stopped us from running, and running was what caused many people to die.

My son, who was eight years old at the time, was a fighter. On the day that the women ravaged the food from the priest's wife, he provided me some food he hid away.

I offer some of the food to my mother-in-law. She said, "No, I am not hungry." I encouraged her to take some bread, but it would take multiple tries to get her to eat. My mother-in-law was very sensitive and emotional. She was orphaned during World War II— she, along with her twin sister witnessed her parents' throats being cut. Now, she was living a new hell.

I had not yet told her that her son died, and how it happened. I kept the secret long after the war, as I could not come to terms with telling her. I loved her too much to cause so much pain at a time when she needed to be strong. Even though my mother-in-law never really liked me as her daughter-in-law, I carried the burden of my husband's death so that she would not have to bear it. Deep inside our souls, we were far apart, but we were bonded through our love for my husband and my son.

No Immunity in a Holocaust

One night, the doors popped open. One of the women was so scared, she accidently kicked me hard, making it hard to me to breathe. A flashlight shined on us, and the guards said, "You, you and you—follow me." One of the women they selected was A.H. A guard then beat up a child and asked one of the women, "Where are the keys?" No one knew what the guard meant.

In the second room, they questioned A.H., "Where are the keys?!" The Chetniks had found out S.L., the SDS leader, was helping A.H., and they came to ask for the keys to her car. She said she gave they keys to S.L. They brought S.L. into the room, and he denied that she gave him the keys.

They started to slap and beat her. Again, they said, "Where are the keys?" She said, "I do not know." They punched and beat her again. Once they discovered that she did in fact have the keys, they took her away. The note that was given to her never provided immunity.

Her kids cried out for her. One of the guards said, "Somebody take her kids, or I am going to kill them." A woman in the room tried to comfort them, but the children still cried and screamed as the guards dragged A.H. by her hair out of the room. She survived this ordeal and she now lives in Sarajevo, but she has never spoken about what happened to her on that day.

The Cross We Carry

The scars of war leave indelible images that last a lifetime. Living through the camps and holocaust left me with emotional scars as well as physical ones. Cuts and burns are part of the torture in a camp, but the lasting scars are the ones triggered by the trauma.

On my right arm, I have a cross that was carved into my arm that was meant to degrade me as a Muslim. It was carved after I was sexually assaulted, so that I would remember the event. But to me, that cross represents hope, not fear. Just like the star and crescent symbol, the cross represents peace, happiness, and faith.

The solider who gave me the scar was someone I knew. He was in his thirties, and he gave an order to a younger solider to rape me. I was seven months pregnant at the time. I was taken by the younger solider while my son was sleeping, and he told me to make something on the stove for the Chetniks.

Many of the Chetnik soldiers had to follow rules they did not understand, including this younger solider. His boss, the older solider, came in and asked if the coffee was done. He then said to the younger soldier, "Have you ever been with a woman? Because now is your chance."

The young soldier felt awful that he had to do this to me. He resisted the order to rape me at first, which resulted in his superiors violently kicking me across the room to show their frustration. The young solider did not rape me because he was inhumane—he raped me because that was what was expected of him. He is likely still haunted to this day over what he was made to do.

I wasn't worried for myself so much as I was concerned about my baby in the womb being safe. I was also concerned for the safety of my son back at the church. I was in survival mode, and my mother's instinct was taking over. My goal was to stay alive because I needed to protect my unborn baby and my older son. I did not feel humiliated, nor did I feel a loss of dignity, and that is still true today.

Exploding Cow

Across the street from the church, I saw my neighbor's house was in flames. The Serbian soldiers said sarcastically, "Who did that?" We heard in the distance commanders giving orders to their soldiers. We start to wonder what was going on.

An old man called Uncle L was giving command to cows and kettles (baby cows). We realize that he was the one who started the fires. A cow that was burning in one of the fires exploded. Uncle L took his rifle and shot the other cows.

The cruelty of the war extended to animals. My heart ached to witness the animal abuse. I could not understand why they would take their anger out on a cow. A cow provides milk, and just because a Muslim owns the cow, that does not make the cow Muslim.

When the kids saw Uncle L, they ran inside. Our fear bothered him, and he yelled, "Don't run from Uncle L!" I told my son to get in the house, but I was frozen in the doorway from the horror of what was going on, so instead I watched him.

Uncle L approached the house. His appearance was scary and created a cloud of fear in us. He was dressed in all black and had a long gray beard. He wore a Chetnik hat, called a kokarda, with an emblem on it. He had munitions in the shape of an "X" across his chest, ready to be used in his machine gun. He had the eyes of a killer—bloodshot and crazy. In his belt was a bottle of Bosnian tequila. He reeked of alcohol.

We were so prepared to die, we came out of the house as he requested. I knew his son, and I had attended the funeral of his son just prior to the war. His son died while participating in the ethnic cleansing in Croatia prior to the war. He yelled at us that we were guilty of the death of his son.

Uncle L's anger towards us reflected the root cause of the death of his son—religious intolerance. But death does discriminate based on religion. It is humans that choose to discriminate based on ideologies passed down from generation to generation.

The Human Shield

When you live in a concentration camp, so many memories stem from the deaths that you witness. I can vividly remember all the human beings that were killed in front of me. There was a point in the war where I stood behind a human shield and watched everyone die all at once. I witnessed the murder of a mother and her friend, both shot in the heart. It was a gruesome act.

I never thought the human shield would actually protect me. I thought my role would be to protect others, including my children. As the firing squad approached, they screamed caustic comments, calling the women bitches and hookers. As horrific as the comments were, the actions of the soldiers only enhanced the importance of saving my children.

I knew that saving my son and the baby in my womb required important choices at a moment's notice. On that day, I turned my back to the firing line to save my son. I positioned myself so that if I died, at least my son would live. I had to stay focused and give my son instructions on what to do after I died. There is a journey into one's soul that happens when you have only seconds to plan in hopes that one person survives.

Bus to Hell

The Chetniks announced that we would be transported in buses to Zepa. Zepa was a three-hour drive from where we were. We were told to pack and be ready within 24 hours.

When the buses arrived, I heard a Serbian soldier whisper something to a woman, and she exited the bus. Instinctively, I knew we should not go. The Serbs claimed they were taking us to a hostage exchange for their soldiers, but the truth was the buses were a one-way ticket to ethnic cleansing. Most women charged onto the bus, thinking this was their opportunity to escape the holocaust. Little did they know it would only bring death.

Thirteen of us stayed in the priest's house. All of us survived based on our instincts that something was not right. By staying back, it saved my child's and mother-in-law's lives.

Any changes that came, I would watch for the soldiers' reactions to my fellow Bosnians. The site of panic on their faces gave me all the details I would need to survive.

Later on, I was made to enter a bulletproof van that moved us across town. As we drove, I bore witness to the death and peril that was happening. The Serbs left bodies in the front yards of their victim's houses. I peeked out the machine gun window as we passed by Bird Hill. This would be the last time I would see this special place from my youth.

We ended up in front of my old high school, which had been converted into a Muslim refugee camp. There, I saw many familiar faces. My brother's best friend was in the camp, wearing a uniform and holding a machine gun. My friend Sylvia[11] was also in the camp. She brought me into the building.

Sylvia and her family, who were Catholic, were living in the library of the school. The family provided us with hot water from a stove to bathe. They were very generous. There were lots of refugees there working together to survive. Many of them gave up some of their sustenance so that we could survive.

We had been assigned to the chemistry lab upstairs. The room was shared by refugees that lost everything, including their family members. We were given blankets, and my child and mother-in-law fell asleep.

That first night, the sadness hit me very hard. Instead of going to sleep, I walked the halls. Each classroom was packed with refugees. You could look out the windows and witness hell, because only hell could look and sound like this. We heard screaming, yelling, grenades, and gunfire. Everything was burning.

In the morning, we could hear throughout the school people fighting over who could use the stove. There were around 300 of us there. We were reassured that there were buses coming, and we would be taken to Olovo, a free territory between the Serbian and Bosnian armies.

---

[11] Author's Note—Shortly before writing this book, Mance found out through the war crimes prosecutor that Sylvia has cancer. Sylvia was too ill to testify.

"Put on Your Pants!"

My mother-in-law had a bad habit of refusing to wear pants. She was too proud and wore dresses due to cultural norms. I would tell her all the time, "Put on your pants!"

One day, some of the Chetniks came to school. We were told we would soon be transported on a bus. Some of the refugees did not want to go on the buses, but those who stayed would regret this. They were raped, tortured, and killed. My instincts would once again save us.

When the buses arrived, I grabbed my son and mother-in-law, and we boarded the bus. I sat behind the driver with my son, and my mother-in-law sat behind me. This was strategic on my part so I could be near the machine gun in front of the bus.

When we passed a brewery, I thought we were heading for the men's concentration camp. I thought about grabbing the machine gun and killing as many Chetniks as I could. But I had second thoughts about the plan. I looked over to my child and realized my son would be in jeopardy if I went for the gun[12].

The bus ride was seven hours long. We arrived in the middle of a dark forest, close to dusk. They told us to get out. One of the military police officers on the bus was a former friend from high school, named Mladen. He had a rifle, which we knew he was about to use to shoot us. One of the elderly ladies passed him as she exited and said, "Listen Mladen, I wish you a long life,

---

[12] Author's Note—What we learn from this part of trauma is the ability to use your brain to control fear is what can possibly determine a person's ability to live. The ability to utilize the intellectual reservoir during a crisis is important. Once the brain shuts down, it is more likely for death to occur.

and for me, death, so that you can live and think what you did."
It was so powerful, it gave me goosebumps then, and still does
today.

There were about 300 of us altogether. I grabbed my son and
mother-in-law, and I told them to get out quickly and run. As I
pushed my mother-in-law and son along as best I could, I heard
rapid gunfire. I turned around, and I watched as people started
to fall like trees in the forest. My mother-in-law groaned as if
she was shot, but then said, "I am in poison ivy." Even during
this darkest of time, I laughed uncontrollably. I knew she should
have worn those damn pants!

Those who survived, including the three of us, waited in the
dark of the forest. Another bus arrived, but this time, it was a
Bosnian army bus to take us to the free territory in the city of
Olovo. They were there to rescue us.

From Rescue to Refugee

We were brought to the village and instructed to find a house that we could stay in. I found an elderly family, and they provided me with the opportunity to wash our clothes. My son was given some things to wear, even though they were too big.

Soon, we heard a knock at the door. A loud voice told us we needed to pack and run back to the bus. My mother-in-law had her dress on, but my clothes were drying above the stove. The woman of the house gave me her clothes to wear, and I left mine behind, still wet on the clothesline.

We ran back to the bus. We were instructed to be quiet as we were approaching Chetnik check points. When finally arrived at our destination, we were put up in a hotel.

At the hotel, I started bleeding from my pregnancy. I was provided a doctor, and he injected me with antibiotics to help reduce the bleeding. The bleeding soon stopped.

After two days in a hotel, the buses brought us to the city of Visoko. I was kind of excited since the city was not too far from my grandparents' hometown. When we arrived in Visoko, we settled down in a gym. We used the mats left behind as our beds. While there, we had to go through a series of interviews as they investigated the mass genocide.

During this time, my mother-in-law started to distance herself from me. I told her to pack her stuff because my cousins from Fojnica were picking us up. She coldly said, "No, I am not going with you." My neighbors were trying to convince her to go with them to another town in central Bosnia instead of travelling with me.

I felt like she was starting to realize that her son was dead. I realized that this could be the last time I was with her, so I told her, "That's okay." And that was the end of our time together.

I sent a message to my first cousins, who I had not seen in years. They had a meeting prior to my arrival, where they discussed what they would do with me when I arrived, especially since I was pregnant. One uncle did not want to take me in. Another aunt wanted to share responsibility of me week to week. My cousin Amir, who had been on the frontline of the war, said, "No, she is not a gypsy. I will not allow her to go house to house. She has gone through enough."

No one wants a refugee, but Amir's experiences taught him that taking me into his house was right thing to do. This was so powerful and meant the world to me. For the first time, I felt like someone wanted me, which was a new feeling for me.

My cousin Amir was so wonderful, and I was thankful. I felt safe with Amir, and so I stayed with him for a year. Amir became my younger son's godfather, as he saved his life. To this day, I have great love and admiration for Amir's generosity, and we still keep in touch.

The Birth of Elvedin

I found myself alone in the house when the contractions started. Amir was working, and so I had to walk to the hospital on my own. I ducked and hid from men as I journeyed to the hospital.

At the hospital, I gave birth to my son without any medical examination beforehand. They put me on the table, and I delivered a health, eight-pound baby amidst the chaos that surrounded me.

I shared my hospital room with two other ladies—one was Catholic, and the other was Muslim. Tensions would flare between the two women. It was very weird to give birth as a refugee and be smack in the middle of these warring factions.

Ironically, the Catholic woman was kind to me and shared her food, but the Muslim woman treated me quite differently. Even though we shared the same religion, she would talk down to me or talk as if I was not there. In her mind, refugees were the bottom of the caste system. I felt like I was not even a person when I was in her presence.

The Muslim lady enjoyed that I was alone in the hospital. She tried to shame me by pointing out my shortcomings. She would say, "Oh, who is going to pick you up?" Then she bragged about her husband coming to get her, and how lucky she was to have her husband and such luxuries.

But the Muslim lady's husband was late picking her up, which was embarrassing to her. Meanwhile, Amir came with a friend to pick me up in his Mercedes. He brought me a bouquet of flowers and put money under my son's pillow, which is a Bosnian tradition. When the Muslim woman realized that I was being picked up in a Mercedes, she became angry. It was

unacceptable in her world that I would leave in such a nice car
with a huge bouquet of flowers, and she would not.

Reuniting with my Brother

I had assumed up until this point that my brother was dead, but I soon learned that he was alive, which was an amazing surprise. While he was hiding in the woods, he had been hit by a grenade and was thrown into a tree, but he survived.

To escape the war, my brother embarked on a 24-hour journey through rough terrain. He travelled by horse and at night over the mountain of Grebak, crossing enemy lines. This was the only route to free territory.

He wound up in a war hospital located in the middle of the woods next to Sarajevo. He was then transferred to my husband's hometown, the city of Gorazde, which was the only town that was free in East Bosnia. It is now known as "Hero Town" as it was the only town to survive the ethnic cleansing. My in-laws live there still.

I had not seen my brother for a year. When I arrived at the hospital, his injuries were quite serious, and he could barely walk. I let my brother know I had a baby, then I asked him, "Why are you not walking?" He let me know that the grenade had hit him severely in his privates. We exchanged laughter from the story.

My brother's hospital roommate was a Croatian solider. He had bandages around his head. I asked, "What happened to him?" My brother said, "He hurt himself playing Russian Roulette," and laughed his ass off at his joke.

When my brother was released from the hospital, we both moved to Fojnica[13].

---

[13] Author's Note—We wrote this chapter during the 28th anniversary of the Bosnian genocide.

Hospital Conflicts

Living through genocide, you experience daily pain. The pain can be physical or emotional. Even experiences with family can cause tensions to run higher than normal. Family can no longer trust each other. For this reason, when I would ask for help, I wouldn't receive it.

My newborn son struggled to survive. I learned that he was suffering from dehydration and would die if I did not find medical help, which meant travelling to the city of Zenica, where the clinical center for Central Bosnia was located.

At the hospital, children were chosen for care based on a lottery system. Because of this, my child and I were disregarded while others were treated. It caused so much hurt, seeing other mothers receive care for their children while my child suffered.

Wounded soldiers started to appear in the hospital as control of the city passed to Catholic mercenaries. My nine-year-old son was captured since no one in my family took care of him while I was at the hospital with my baby. All of this was too heavy for me to comprehend.

While in the hospital, I sat in a hallway. On the first day, there was gentlemen there that was not very friendly. He was a crisis staff that was supposed to help patients, but he did absolutely nothing.

On the second day, I spoke to another crisis staff that came from a mixed marriage. I told him what was going on, and how long I'd been sitting in the hallway. He became so enraged over what was happening to me, he went into the hospital and demanded that I be treated with respect. He also reached out to Equilbiri in France to help find my older son.

I was then given lodging and help. Equilibri found my older son in a concentration camp, but my younger son was so sick, we had to stay in the hospital for the following month. During our stay, I volunteered to help bring in patients that arrived daily. The hospital was short-staffed due to the war.

Soon, I would see familiar faces. One day, I was making a bed for a patient, and the man yelled, "Don't touch me!" I turned the man over, and it was my cousin. He grew up as a communist, and so I knew his response to me touching me was caused by communist indoctrination regarding women and their place in society. Through my volunteer work, I would be a witness to the horrors of war once again.

Working With Special Needs

After I left the hospital and moved back to Fojnica, I returned to being a refugee. I was homeless and confused about what I should do next. Eventually, I found a rundown, abandoned house to live in. I had to use humanitarian donations to survive. The lines to receive the donations were long and dangerous. Little did I know, the humanitarian center would change my life forever.

While in line humanitarian center, I heard there was an institution for kids and adults with special needs, called "Backovici in Zavod Drin Fojinca." They were looking for help because they had 400 patients with special needs that were left alone. The staff felt overwhelmed, and some had run away. The abandoned patients were alone and lacking any type of care. The director, K.P., was guided by the Croatian Defense Council and the army. While neither entity allowed her to physically go in to work, she would go into the community to find volunteers. This is how we met.

I volunteered through Canada's United Nations Protection Force (UNPROFOR). If you worked for UNPROFOR, you would be paid with food rations. Every morning, the Canadians would pick us up in a transporter, and we would go through the checkpoints to get to work. The Canadians would guide us to ensure safe travel.

The institution had a wide range of people with disabilities, but all of them were in need of help. When I first arrived, I found the patients in chains. Without medications or staff, the chain were how they were kept safe.

UNPROFOR had us provide cooking for the patients and take care of their dietary needs. They also taught us how to take care of wounds and provide injections to patients. I learned how to take care of patients with very limited resources. Self-care items such as shampoo and soap were often consumed by the patients, which was confusing to us volunteers.

UNPROFOR would achieve peacekeeping success in 1995, resulting in about 350 residents at the facility being transferred to other institutions in Bosnian territory. An institution called Drin would be become my new workplace. I served as a head nurse for the night shift.

During the day, I spent time with my two sons. I would see many refugees, mostly mothers, that were helpless. I started an association for victims of the war. I acquired a sponsor, World Vision International in the United States. They were the first organization to feed and provide clothing and food to the refugees.

Working nights and raising children during the day would take a toll. It was two full-time jobs. During this time, I earned an Occupational Therapy certification, which allowed me to work the day shift. But even so, peace in the region would reduce donations and require the government to pay us less for our work. The pay became too low, and I struggled living on a reduced monthly paycheck.

Additionally, my older son was struggling with passing school, and the teacher tried to pressure me to pay him for tutoring so that he could graduate. I gave the teacher 10 BAMs (Bosnian marks) for tutoring, but the money did not change anything. I had to go down to the school and physically intimidate the teacher to pass my son.

After four years in my position at work, I could not pay for my apartment and provide for my family. In 2000, when my sons were 8 and 18 years old, we were evicted.

No One Loves a Refugee

When you are a refugee, no one wants to have anything to do with you. After the war, my family would forget I was family. My mom's family did not speak to me after the concentration camps. Some of them even today want nothing to do with me.

I had to make a choice. I knew the Bosnians no longer had a homeland like they had before the war. Even being called a refugee there was a sign of disrespect, as though we were to blame for starting the war. I was without a home, and I felt the U.S. was the only way to salvage my life after the concentration camps.

I had to escape again, since it was better for me to be a refugee in the United States versus a refugee in my own country. I applied for an immigration visa to work in the United States. It would take nine months before I received a response.

As I planned for us to go to the United States, without me knowing it, my older son reconnected with his father. His father sent him money to earn his trust and friendship. My son was using the money, as some teenagers would do, to explore habits like smoking and recreational drugs. These addictions would become a lifetime struggle for my son.

By the time my visa was approved, my son had become alienated from me, and my ex-husband refused to allow him to go to the United States. My ex-husband was still angry at me over the divorce, and he knew that keeping my son in Bosnia would deeply hurt me. When we spoke, he said, "I cannot give him up, it is too early for him to go."

I felt held hostage to the timeline I had to follow to leave the country, and the demands my son's father was placing on me. If missed my chance to leave the country, I might not get another one.

My ex-husband's stubbornness led to my son staying with his father. Moving to the United States without my older son left a hole in my heart. This guilt has stayed with me for my entire adult life. I will wake up only to immediately think of the emptiness felt by not being able to help my son.

The protective barrier I provided for my son left with me on that on a plane. Without my guidance, my son struggled, which was painful to witness. The rejection and denial from my son's father's family was just as hurtful. The changes in my son were not something they felt any responsibility to acknowledge. Instead, they pointed to the emotional trauma from our time together in Bosnia as the source of my son's problems.

My son would only live with my ex-husband for a year. His father threw him out of the house shortly after I left. The many years that followed were not easy. My son went into rehab many times, and each time hurt me.

At times, I blamed my husband for the failures in my son's life. Today, I forgive him. I recognize that he was raised to believe that a woman's only role was to be obedient, and that raising a child is entirely on the mother. Divorce was a slap in the face to him, which is why he was so vengeful towards me. He could not see how his decisions would ultimately punish my son more than me.

What hurts me more now is that my son thinks the same way as his father. Now that my son has children of his own, I worry that history will repeat itself.

The Road to the United States

Despite what you hear on the news, it is not an easy road for refugees to come to the United States. I had to complete a series of tests to qualify for immigration. The application is quite lengthy, and there is a review process with an investigation to prove that a person is who they say they are on the application.

Once the application is approved, you go through an interview process. Then, there is a three-day seminar to earn a certificate. The seminar provides an English language lesson and cultural symbols that are important to learn. The final step is passing a drug test.

After going through this process, I was assigned to move to Upstate NY. It was the first time I did not have to worry about someone punching me or witnessing daily violence. Peace had come with my new home.

After years of sleep deprivation, the comfort of being safe caused me to oversleep and miss my ride to the airport. The last flight for Syracuse left without me and my younger son, so we took a flight to New York City instead. When I arrived at JFK airport, I kissed the ground that I would eventually call home.

We went to a hotel that served us a huge meal. Everything seemed generous compared to what I had known before. Meanwhile, the Refugee Center in Utica, NY, was worried when I hadn't arrived with the other refugees. Our host located us in NYC and brought us back to Syracuse. My cousins that arrived ahead of me then brought us to Utica.

I had an apartment ready for me when I arrived in Utica. I applied for benefits to pay back the Lutheran Church that sponsored my ticket. In order to earn benefits, refugees are required to attend eight hours a day at a school for English as a Second Language.

My son started school. This was the first time I experienced a school bus. It was also the first time I could trust my child to be away from me for extended periods of time.

The Refugee Center provided job support. My first job was at the Presbyterian Nursing Home in Utica. The director of the nursing home was a man named Mr. Salerno. His son was a priest that would visit the nursing home. It was a great first job, as the patients needed love and hope. The American staff and patients understood that I was a refugee and that I was still learning English, and they respected my work ethic.

Ironically, though, the other Bosnian staff mocked me. The bullying was so significant that I would hide from them during work. Mr. Salerno pulled me aside one day after he noticed I was crying. He said, "Never forget, they can do whatever they want, but who is laughing last?" This was his way of reinforcing that I would succeed. He also thanked me for my work.

His generosity would continue after this incident. He said he would help me learn English since this was the primary source of the bullying from the other Bosnians. He worked with me, and I improved my language skills. This led me to become a Certified Nursing Assistant.

Other opportunities led me to my passion, which is cooking. The local casino, Turning Stone, hired me to work with their cooking staff who were primarily Bosnian. I was the supervisor of the kitchens, and I managed the different restaurants at the casino.

My hours were 8pm-3am. This was perfect for many of the Bosnians there since they were hard-working people. While I loved the job, the hours were very tough for me. I couldn't sleep when I got home because I had to send my son to school in the mornings. This disparity would cause me to leave the casino and head back to college.

I went to school to learn more about working with children that have special needs. In order to go to college, refugees have to go through ESL classes before they can enroll. This can be time-consuming. My ESL classes went on for two years.

My first job after I finished was a job at Upstate Cerebral Palsy. My recruiter was Nicole Maneen. She sent me for an interview at a residential program for children with special needs in Utica, NY. When I started working there, I felt this overwhelming feeling that I was home. That was 15 years ago, and I still call Upstate Cerebral Palsy my home today.

Everything I Could Never Have Before

Happy endings can happen even to the most traumatized soul. I am a living example that blessings can come from a cursed life. In the United States, I met the love of my life, a man named Keith. We have been together for over 20 years.

Keith is the positive relationship that I have always been searching to find. Keith is a private man, and so this chapter is short and simple. Soul mates are real, and they can come into your life when you least expect it.

Giving a Kidney

As I settled in the United States, I found out that my brother needed my help back in Bosnia. Both his impacted kidneys were starting to fail, and his health had been affected by living in sub-standard housing for years. He had been found unconscious in his apartment. He needed a kidney transplant to save his life, but at the time, there was nothing I could do to help him as I did not have the financial resources.

By 2007, I had met the love of my life, and my financial situation had improved. When I called my brother to tell him I could help him, he interrupted me, crying, "I lost both my kidneys and I have to go on dialysis." He thought it was too late for him to have the transplant. I told him, "I will give you a kidney. I am here for you."

I asked my supervisor at my job if I could take a leave of absence so that I could return to Bosnia to offer my brother a kidney to save his life. The Human Resource Department was amazing. They supported my leave of absence, which meant the world to me.

Helping my brother was important because saving his life was symbolic to me and helped to heal some of emotional wounds. Nobody had been there to help me, so I found value in being able to help my brother. It is so much easier to do good things when you've suffered and lived in misery. I choose to be a better person because of the trauma I've experienced.

The return to Bosnia also allowed me the opportunity to tell my younger son about the complications of my past family relationships. I was able to reconnect with people, including my Russian language teacher, who visited me while I was in the hospital. My son met his paternal grandparents, and I was able to finally tell them how their son died. I was freed from the burden of keeping this secret, and from the pain and suffering it caused me.

Witness to a Holocaust

My past would have to be reconciled while living in Upstate NY. A phone call came one day from a lawyer. He was a prosecutor for the war crimes committed in Bosnia. He had learned that I was a witness to the crimes against humanity that had occurred there. I was a part of history, and my story needed to be told.

The focus of the war crimes was my hometown of Rogatica. Our small neighborhood of Gracanica saw some of the worse crimes against humanity, and what occurred was beyond any of our comprehension. The prosecutor in Bosnia learned that I was the only one during the time of atrocities who kept a journal of the events as they happened in June 1992.

Once the prosecutor learned about me and what I had witness, it helped to hold people accountable for the crimes they perpetrated.

Adding Guardian Angels

Our school nurse, Ms. D, became one of my guardian angels. Unfortunately, prior to finishing this book, she ended up leaving our school. She was the type of person that checked on me daily, as well as everyone else in the building. She spent more time in classrooms instead of her office.

Every day, Ms. D would come into the school kitchen, which I oversee, and warm up her tea. She would use this time to check in on me and my health issues. I thought it was a clever and caring approach, using her tea as an excuse to see me. It that demonstrated how much she cared for me.

Ms. D is a kind and empathetic person that impacted my life. Her job was a calling, and more than a paycheck to her. When people are surrounded by guardian angels, they heal. Ms. D understood that.

In the darkness, we look for light, and there we find guardian angels everywhere when we choose to look for them. Connectivity is the key to mental health, and finding our guardian angels is the key to overcoming our demons.

Losing Guardian Angels

Guardian angels can also leave a person's life. It is never easy. There were two people from my job at UCP that mean a great deal to me, named Mathew and Linley. They were a couple, whose relationship was inspired by their work with children with disabilities. They shared a common passion together that was quite special.

Unfortunately, due to a tragic car accident, Mathew lost his life, which was unexpected and traumatic. Everyone was caught by surprise. When I opened the door that day and saw everyone was crying, I thought that our principal's mother had passed after a long-term illness[14].

The shock of Mathew's death took my breath away, leaving me feeling paralyzed. In that moment, my crying was not just for Mathew—it was for everyone that I had lost in my lifetime.

I had to go home after I found out the news. My body experienced the pain of my past combined with the pain of my present. The death of a friend is a reminder of the genocides that exist in our world. The unexpected loss of life happens on so many levels.

When families are destroyed by a holocaust, new friendships replace the now fractured family unit. The new friendships provide a safety net that had previously been destroyed. This is why people's reactions to death can be so different. Trauma allows a person to feel love and pain in a much different way.

I have high praise for our division Vice President and Senior Vice President and their actions on the day of Mathew's death. I

---

[14] Author's Note—I was there that day after Mathew died. There was a solid wall of staff down that hall. It reminded me of the human shield. Only this time, the human shield was guided by compassion, not hate.

remember how in that moment, all of us became simply human beings, regardless of title or position. When you strip away at what makes us different versus what makes us the same, it is important to recognize compassion as the most decent common element in all of us.

My Heroes Today

There are several people whom I consider my heroes today, and who had an impact on my life.

Ben Ferencz

I have a strong connection to Ben Ferencz. Ben was a war crimes lawyer. Ben was a prosecutor at the War Crimes Tribunal for Nazi Germany. Those hearings taught him that what you see, you cannot unsee. When he saw the concentration camps in Germany, it stayed with him the rest of his life.

Ben is five feet tall, and he needed to stand on books at Nuremberg to speak as a prosecutor. At 100 years of age, Ben still fights war crimes. While his work was primarily in the 20th century, it is more relevant than ever.

Barbara Bush

Admiration for another individual should never be held hostage by your political affiliation. I greatly admire people on both sides of the aisle, including Michelle Obama and Barbara Bush. In particular, I became connected to a book Mrs. Bush wrote. Within the stories in that book, she wrote about the loss of her child. The loss of a child is one that can only be understood by parents who have gone through similar experiences. This is why I'm appreciative of the fact that Barbara Bush wrote about her loss. It helps others heal and realize they are not alone.

Angelina Jolie

Angelina Jolie made a movie in Bosnia that was a fictional account of the war. The movie "In the Land of Blood and Honey" was an example of art imitating life. Ms. Jolie speaks to what this book is trying to do. She wanted to learn more about the holocaust and immersed herself in what happened in Bosnia.

The story told in "In the Land of Blood and Honey" is very familiar to me and my life. The main character is named Ajla, a Muslim Bosnian woman who falls in love with Danijel, a Serbian soldier, prior to the war. Once the war starts, she is betrayed and kidnapped by him, purely because of ethnic differences. But even during the war, she still loved him.

I admire the fact that Angelina Jolie wanted to tell this story. I would love to meet Jolie one day to tell her thank you.

Author's Afterword

Someone that lives a cursed life experiences trauma at all stages of development. Part of what makes Mance so unique is her trauma started at an early age in her life, and the impact of previous experiences can uniquely impact adult trauma. She lived a difficult life leading up the war and holocaust. While there was some happiness, and she did feel loved by her parents, living with parents who were incapable of understanding each other led to hardship for their children.

Today, Mance focuses on the love provided by her parents. She understands that given the proper resources and help, her relationship with her parents could have been different. While the scars ran deep, they healed. Resiliency and hope replace the trauma over time. Part of resiliency is acknowledging and forgiving what has already happened, no matter how long ago.

Without resiliency, people tend to self-medicate to bury the pain caused by trauma, as is the case with Mance's older son. During the course of writing this book, Mance's son went missing in Bosnia, and she feared he was dead. Towards the end of writing this book, she located her son in the same hospital where she found her brother during the war. Her son, struggling with addiction, was offered addiction counseling and recovery services.

It is important for all survivors of trauma to understand the effect of significant events in their lives. Without finding a path to connect to the past, people are held hostage to their personal history and cannot develop coping mechanisms. There is a foundation that is stripped away when trauma occurs that must be regained. Rebuilding that foundation means relinquishing the past abuse and embracing the blessings of life.

Life is never pain free. For some, more than others, people can have private trauma that never comes to light. Yes, there is trauma from concentration camps. It can also come our homes. It does not matter the setting—trauma is very real and very damaging. Mance forgave her parents, but it is harder to forget.

When Mance moved to the United States, one of her coworkers hung himself because he could not talk about his personal trauma. Another coworker that was friends with him stated he had called her the night before to have a cup of coffee, but she had other obligations that night. He never showed signs that he was going to take his life. She cried at work, feeling guilt over not having that cup of coffee with him, and wondering if she could have prevented his death.

The tears from her coworker were new to Mance, and she realized that it was okay to cry in the United States. Have you ever known someone that never could show their feelings? There is a reason for that. Traumatized individuals may never learn how to self-regulate their emotions, only to control them. This is a wall that can seem insurmountable for many. The pain of trauma can create complex anxieties over simple tasks, like entering a room full of people they do not know.

Another part of healing is learning from the trauma. The pathways to resiliency are built upon the pathways of understanding traumatic experiences. The sharing of stories like Mance's help others to learn and understand trauma, whether or not they've experienced it themselves.

Trying to help someone deal with trauma is complicated. Loved ones struggle to understand how trauma impacts us individually, and that's okay. It is tough to walk in the shoes of those that have life experiences different than our own, but learning about these experiences can help us to be more compassionate.

Today, people living in poor countries around the world experience intolerances that lead to death. The media rarely focuses on the unseen carnage that exists in other countries. We repeat these crimes against humanity when we do not embrace the refugees that come to our shores, and instead demonize them as a threat.

Mance's story can also help teachers and social workers understand how trauma plays a role in the classroom. It is our hope that the stories inspire current and future educators to expand their horizons of understanding what impacts learners in their classrooms daily. Some teachers or social workers may assume that coping skills develop quickly. Worse, they think that instead of nurturing the child, their role is to use "tough love" to instill resiliency in the child.

As a former teacher and current school administrator, I can tell you the damage caused by trauma is more severe than we realize. When a child goes through a traumatic event, it can take years to heal. Teachers and social workers can cause more harm when they immediately push coping strategies onto the child.

Sometimes, the champions for children are the adults who learned that empathy is the most powerful tool for learning, and that nurturing is not "giving a child a break." What it does mean is that we recognize what makes us all human, which means loving others as we would want to be loved.

The final part of the healing process is moving forward with purpose. Helping others is good for the soul. Every person that died in front of Mance was a reason to help people with special needs. Every exploding cow was a reason for her to love stray pets in her neighborhood. For Mance, taking care of others is a path to salvation.

When a child or adult fails to heal from trauma, it color the
entirety of the life, affecting everything they do in a negative
manner. But acknowledging the trauma, learning from it, and
moving forward with purpose can help those with trauma heal,
and can create something beautiful from the horrors of their
past. Some may be born into a cursed life, but if you can break
being held hostage by it, you can achieve a blessed life.